TEACHING SCIENCE IN THE BLOCK

Alvin M. Pettus

Myron E. Blosser

EYE ON EDUCATION
6 DEPOT WAY WEST, SUITE 106
LARCHMONT, NY 10538
(914) 833–0551
(914) 833–0761 fax
www.eyeoneducation.com

Library of Congress Cataloging-in-Publication Data

Pettus, Alvin M.
    Teaching science in the block / by Alvin M. Pettus and Myron E. Blosser.
        p.   cm. — (Teaching in the block)
    Includes bibliographical references.
    ISBN 1-930556-08-X
    1. Science—Study and teaching (Secondary). 2. Block scheduling (Education) I. Blosser, Myron E., 1961– II. Title. III. Series.

Q181 .P358   2001
507'.1'273—dc21

                                                                                    00-049590

10 9 8 7 6 5 4 3 2 1

Editorial and production services provided by
Richard H. Adin Freelance Editorial Services
52 Oakwood Blvd., Poughkeepsie, NY 12603-4112
(914-471-3566)

Banishing Anonymity:
Middle and High School Advisement Programs
by John Jenkins and Bonnie Daniel

Constructivist Strategies: Meeting Standards
and Engaging Adolescent Minds
by Chandra Foote, Paul Vermette, and Catherine Battaglia

Collaborative Learning in Middle and
Secondary Schools: Applications and Assessments
by Dawn Snodgrass and Mary Bevevino

Personalized Instruction:
Changing Classroom Practice
by James Keefe and John Jenkins

English Teacher's Guide to Performance
Tasks and Rubrics: Middle School
by Amy Benjamin

English Teacher's Guide to Performance
Tasks and Rubrics: High School
by Amy Benjamin

Developing Parent and Community
Understanding of Performance-Based Assessment
by Kathryn Anderson Alvestad

A Collection of Performance Tasks and Rubrics
Middle School Mathematics
by Charlotte Danielson

High School Mathematics
by Charlotte Danielson and Elizabeth Marquez

High School English Teacher's Guide to Active Learning
by Victor and Marc Moeller

Middle School English Teacher's Guide to Active Learning
by Marc and Victor Moeller

Directory of Programs for Students at Risk
by Thomas L. Williams

The Interdisciplinary Curriculum
by Arthur K. Ellis and Carol J. Stuen

The Paideia Classroom: Teaching for Understanding
by Terry Roberts with Laura Billings

DEDICATIONS

To my mother, Julia Mary Moss Pettus, for providing encouragement and support for many years and serving as a role model for her eight children in valuing honesty and determination. To the memory of my father, Willie Clay Pettus, whose work ethic endures as a guide.

Alvin

To my parents, Glendon L. and Dorothy N. Blosser, who cultivated within me the love of wonder and opened our home to and encouraged my early attempts at practicing the scientific method. To my students, who have been my best teachers.

Myron

FOREWORD

Block schedules provide opportunities for teachers to change their instructional strategies so that students become more active and successful learners. There is a growing body of evidence from experiences with high school and middle school scheduling that strongly supports the notion that with proper staff development and careful schedule design the overall school environment becomes more positive and productive. There also is evidence that many teachers increase their personal contacts with students. Furthermore, when curricular and instructional issues are addressed appropriately, achievement in many schools improves, as measured by factors such as reduced failure rates, increased numbers of students on honor rolls, and higher test scores.

Because we believe that instructional change is the key to successful block scheduling, we are sponsoring this series of books, written primarily by teachers who have been successful in teaching in block schedules. While we believe this series can be helpful to teachers working in any type of schedule, the ideas should be especially useful for middle and high school teachers who are "Teaching in the Block."

The idea of scheduling middle and high schools in some way other than daily, single periods is not new. We find in educational history numerous attempts to modify traditional schedules and to give the instructional school day greater flexibility. In the 1960s, for example, approximately 15 percent of American high schools implemented modular scheduling, which typically used 15 to 20 modules of time to create instructional periods that varied in length from between 15 minutes to classes of 100 minutes or more.

Many reasons have been given for the demise of modular scheduling as practiced during the 1960s and 1970s; however, two of the primary reasons often cited (Canady and Rettig, 1995, pp. 13-15) are that (1) too much independent study time was included in those schedules and school management became a problem, and (2) teachers in many schools never were assisted in seriously changing classroom instruction in longer periods of time. Current models of block scheduling do not have significant independent study time; therefore, school management problems are reduced, not exacerbated. We have found, however, that in schools where block scheduling has been implemented successfully, considerable attention has been paid to adapting instruction to maximize the potential of available time.

We repeatedly have stated that if schools only "change their bells" block scheduling should not be implemented. We also have contended that if teachers are not provided with extensive staff development, block scheduling will be a problem. "The success or failure of the [current] block scheduling movement will be determined largely by the ability of teachers...to improve instruction.

Regardless of a school's time schedule, what happens between individual teachers and students in classrooms is still most important, and simply altering the manner in which we schedule schools will not ensure better instruction by teachers or increased learning by students" (Canady and Rettig, 1995, p. 240).

In this seventh volume of our *Teaching in the Block* series, entitled *Teaching Science in the Block,* authors Alvin M. Pettus and Myron E. Blosser share their science teaching experiences, which include instructing within a traditional single period schedule, as well as, teaching in the two major types of block schedules—the alternate-day and the 4/4 or semester block schedule.

Collectively the authors have more than 40 years of experience teaching science courses in secondary schools and methods courses at the university level. In addition, the authors have served in science supervisory positions at both state and district levels. Currently, Mr. Blosser is K-12 science coordinator and a science teacher in the Harrisonburg City Schools in Virginia, where he has received both state and national teaching awards. Dr. Pettus is professor and assistant director of the School of Education at James Madison University. Their extensive and varied experiences provide the reader with a wealth of expertise and examples.

The authors begin by describing several different forms of block scheduling and how science instruction may be affected by those schedules. They also identify both the positive aspects of block schedules for science instruction and the challenges of such schedules. With longer blocks of instructional time comes the opportunity for science teachers to use a variety of teaching methodologies. In particular, the larger blocks of time allow the science teacher to provide the type of inquiry and experiential instruction advocated by national science groups and organizations. Accordingly, the science teacher should be able to guide students through a variety of laboratory and investigative learning activities that often are difficult to manage or complete during shorter time periods. The authors state that one of the major challenges of block schedules is the need to compact the science curriculum content so that time truly is available for in-depth learning.

Because block schedules provide extended time, science teachers must utilize a wider range of teaching and assessment strategies in their classrooms. Consequently, the authors illustrate examples of instructional and assessment activities which will assist teachers in becoming facilitators rather than directors of learning and will encourage students to become more engaged in and responsible for their learning.

In addition to providing a variety of instructional activities and examples, the authors also suggest formats for lesson plans; various types of assessments, including sample rubrics for scoring purposes; guides for field trips; suggested computer software; guidelines for using the Internet and electronic mail; and recommended Web sites for general science, biology, chemistry, earth science, physics, and environmental and ecological studies.

While we believe this book will be a useful guide for all science teachers regardless of their school's schedule, it especially will be helpful to middle and high school teachers working in block schedules. The practical strategies provided in this volume will allow science teachers to maximize the potential of the extended time block and place additional emphasis on laboratories, seminars, field investigations, discussions, and use of technology—all critical components of effective science instruction in today's schools.

Robert Lynn Canady
Michael D. Rettig

ACKNOWLEDGMENTS

The authors wish to thank the following people:

- Michael D. Rettig for broaching the idea of writing this book to us and providing encouragement and advice along the way;

- Robert Sickles, publisher, for his patience and support;

- The science teachers at Harrisonburg High School, especially Larry White and Ryan Sensenig, for providing input and reactions upon request;

- Judy Patterson and Denise Snoddy at James Madison University for their secretarial assistance;

- Our wives, Helene and Rhonda, for their patience and support; and

- Our children, Lana, Meta, and Tina Pettus, and Kurtis, Kelsey, and Bryce Blosser for sharing their fathers' time with this project.

TABLE OF CONTENTS

ABOUT THE AUTHORS

Alvin M. Pettus has been a secondary school science teacher, a state-level science supervisor in Virginia, and a college science methods and curriculum instructor. He is currently a professor and assistant director of the School of Education at James Madison University in Harrisonburg, VA. He has served on a local school board and on other local and state-level boards and committees with public education missions. He has written articles and made presentations concerning science instruction, environmental education, and multicultural and diversity education issues. He can be contacted at the School of Education, James Madison University, MSC 1908, Harrisonburg, VA 22807 (pettusam@ jmu.edu).

Myron E. Blosser has taught high school science in the traditional 50-minute, seven periods per day schedule, in an alternate day A/B schedule, and in a 4×4 semester plan schedule. He is currently teaching Honors Biology, Advanced Placement Biology, and Molecular Genetics at Harrisonburg High School and serves as the Harrisonburg City Public Schools K-12 Science Coordinator. He has received a number of awards for his teaching, including the Virginia Association of Science Teachers' Biology Teacher of the Year Award, the National Association of Biology Teachers' Outstanding Biology Teacher of the Year for Virginia, and *USA Today*'s All USA Teacher Team Award. He has been involved in local, state and national curriculum writing efforts in the area of Biology and Biotechnology. He can be contacted at Harrisonburg High School, 395 South High Street, Harrisonburg, Va. 22801 (mblosser@harrisonburg.k12. va.us).

PREFACE

Teaching Science in the Block is designed to assist secondary school science teachers plan and provide quality instruction for students where the class sessions are arranged in blocks of time that are longer than the traditional 40- to 55-minute class sessions. Because quality science instruction for students in longer blocks of time is not significantly different from quality science instruction in traditional schedules, we also invite prospective and practicing science teachers who are using traditional schedules to peruse the information contained in this volume.

This book provides information that describes the structure of block scheduling; informs science teachers of the advantages of teaching in the block; reminds science teachers of the importance of planning, whether teaching in a block schedule or otherwise; and presents ideas for providing science instruction during longer but fewer class sessions. Much of the information is provided in easy-to-follow lists, tables, and charts that can be used as a quick reference and reminder. In some instances, examples of instructional activities and resources are provided to promote interpretation and serve as catalysts for users to develop their own instructional ideas and locate appropriate resources. Because we expect users to include teachers of physical, life, and earth and space sciences, we selected examples from across those broad areas, but we did not make an effort to represent each area under each topic discussed. We are hopeful, however, that teachers in one science area will be able to review examples related to another science area and think of appropriate activities and procedures for instruction in their own area.

We encourage science teachers who are preparing to teach in block schedules to read or peruse the entire volume first to get a sense of the sequence and connectedness of the ideas presented. Beginning with Chapter 1, concerning general and long-term planning, and proceeding through Chapter 2, on short-term planning, Chapter 3, dealing with instructional strategies, and Chapter 4, on evaluation and assessment, the content tends to follow a logical instructional sequence. Chapter 5 describes tools and technologies available to teachers using block schedules. After determining the scope of the information included in the book, individual teachers will be able to refer to specific sections or topics for ideas and hints to plan and implement science instruction in block schedules.

Alvin M. Pettus
Myron E. Blosser

1

STRUCTURES AND ISSUES CONCERNING TEACHING SCIENCE IN THE BLOCK

Many schools have changed, or are transitioning, from a six-, seven-, or eight-period day, consisting of brief class sessions in each curricular area (subject) each day, to block schedules. Schools are adopting schedules that Sharan, Shachar and Levine (1999, 149) refer to as more human centered to support teachers and students and their interaction. Program and curriculum planners for schools are abandoning schedules that require "uniformity dictated by an antiquated conception of institutional organization." They are recognizing the fact that the learning process is one of inquiry and the pursuit of knowledge by students, rather than one of delivery of information to students by teachers.

While the following information and ideas are provided to assist science teachers who are anticipating or already teaching in block-scheduling situations, science teachers using other scheduling arrangements may also find the ideas helpful.

Generally, the effective science teacher:

♦ Knows the content and has planned lessons and instructional units very well

♦ Knows about the students concerning their interests, backgrounds, skills, etc. and how those factors impact the students' learning

♦ Plans, organizes, and teaches to pace and individualize learning activities for students

♦ Communicates and interacts appropriately with students

♦ Recognizes the variety of learning needs of different students and responds positively and sensitively to those learning needs

♦ Has a strong commitment to teaching and helping every student to be successful

♦ Manages the classroom environment, materials, time, and students for attaining learning objectives

- Respects students and conveys that respect and interest in students through actions and speech
- Adopts and uses a variety of teaching approaches and methods for students;
- Monitors student performance and progress consistently, adjusts instruction appropriately, and gives students constructive feedback
- Utilizes the resources of the local, national, and global community
- Networks (communicates) with other professionals (educators and scientists) for professional development

THE LOGISTICS OF TEACHING SCIENCE IN THE BLOCK

In block schedules, students attend three or four class sessions each day. The block schedules are arranged to enable students to study as many subjects per year as they would in a six-, seven-, or eight-period day scheduling format. Canady and Rettig (1996, 2–5) identify some of the reasons schools are abandoning the six-, seven-, or eight-period day schedules. They point out that when students attend six or more classes each day, class periods are so short that:

- Instruction is often fragmented for students.
- An individual teacher may attempt to instruct between 1 and 180 students per day, creating a factory-like and impersonal environment.
- The frequent moving from one class to another promotes more discipline problems and reduces instructional time.
- The options for varying instructional approaches are reduced.
- Teachers find it more difficult to differentiate instruction or accommodate the diverse needs of students.

Block schedules are designed to:

- Reduce the number of classes students must attend and prepare for each day and/or each term
- Allow students variable amounts of time for learning concepts, skills, etc., based on their abilities, learning styles, and interests
- Reduce the number of students teachers must prepare for and interact with each day and/or term
- Reduce the fragmentation inherent in single-period schedules, especially in subjects requiring laboratory work and experiential activities
- Allow and encourage teachers to implement lessons and strategies requiring active student involvement

♦ Reduce the number of class changes (Canady and Rettig, 1996, 6)

Most block schedules that have been implemented follow one of the four basic plans described by Canady and Rettig (1996, 6–20). Variations on the four plans described below may also be workable.

ALTERNATE-DAY SCHEDULE

In alternate-day schedules, classes meet every other day of the school week for extended blocks of time. The amount of time allotted for class sessions depends on the length of the school day and the number of courses students are able to take for the school session. For example, in a 7-hour school day, "a six-course alternate-day schedule usually includes blocks of approximately 120 minutes…." Classes for three courses meet on the first day, and classes for the other three courses meet on the second day. The classes that meet on the first day of a five-day week will meet three times that week and twice the next week. An hour in the middle of the day or some part of it may be used for lunch and/or classes and activities that meet every day. Concerns about alternate-day schedules relate to students' attention spans, teacher planning time, the effects on students' participation in other school activities, and providing for balanced student workloads across the school days. See Canady and Rettig (1996, 6–11).

THE FOUR-BY-FOUR (4/4) SEMESTER PLAN

In the four-by-four semester plan, "students enroll in four courses that meet for approximately 90 minutes per day for the 90 days of a semester. Teachers teach three courses each semester." (Canady and Rettig, 1996, 11)

The advantages of the four-by-four plan are that the teachers work with and keep records for fewer students and fewer classes at one time, enabling them to focus their attention and be more effective. Teachers also have longer planning periods. Students can concentrate on only four courses at a time, with responsibilities for fewer books and other course resources. Common concerns about the four-by-four plan relate to (1) problems students may encounter retaining information between courses because of the time span between some courses, (2) the amount of time actually available for teaching, (3) effects on year-long advanced placement and other courses, and (4) student participation in other school activities (e.g., band and chorus). See Canady and Rettig (1996, 11–16).

TRIMESTER PLANS

In this plan, students take two or three core courses every 60 days (of a 180-day school term) to earn between 6 and 9 credits (or units) per year. Other noncore courses such as band and chorus may be taken throughout the academic year. Extensions and variations in instructional days, length of class periods, and class periods per day can be included to accommodate students who are achieving at different rates or for other reasons. "The benefits and concerns regarding the trimester plans are similar to those identified for the four-by-four plan." (Canady and Rettig, 1996, 16–17).

VARIABLE TERMS PLANS

These plans are similar to the trimester plans, except that the school year is divided "into a combination of long terms and short terms for the purpose of providing instructional time for remediation and enrichment for students." Therefore, the school year may consist of terms of 75 days, 75 days, and 30 days or 75 days, 30 days, and 75 days. Other scheduling plans such as the *alternate-day schedule* and the *four-by-four semester plan* can be combined with the *variable terms plans* to provide more options for students relative to subjects (disciplines) studied, pacing, and other advantages associated with the scheduling plans. See Canady and Rettig, (1996, 17–20).

SCIENCE TEACHING AND
BLOCK SCHEDULING: NATURALLY

If science is taught so students learn through active involvement in learning activities, then teaching in the block is desirable. In the past, schools have tried various scheduling strategies, such as "flexible-modular scheduling," to provide the time and flexibility needed for students to engage in investigations and practice in laboratories and other settings. These scheduling strategies were also designed to allow teachers to employ various instructional methodologies. (Arendt, 1970; Johnson, 1972). The modular scheduling strategies were frequently abandoned after a trial period because they often focused on making changes in specific subjects rather than providing benefits across the entire school curriculum. Block scheduling can be applied across all subject areas and throughout the school to avoid the problems and conflicts of other approaches to scheduling.

Teaching science in a block schedule enables the teacher to use a variety of teaching methodologies. In particular, the larger blocks of time allow the teacher to provide the type of inquiry and experientially based instruction advocated by highly regarded national groups and organizations. Accordingly, the teacher will be able to guide students through a variety of laboratory and investigative learning activities that might be difficult to manage or complete during shorter time blocks. Day, Ivanov, & Binkley (1996) point out the benefits of longer classes for doing laboratory activities.

> We can brief students for a lab activity, perform the experiment, and debrief students all during one class. On the traditional schedule, we often found that students forgot the meaning of the experiment by the next class and were unable to analyze data and draw conclusions. (p. 27)

Day et al. also indicate that in the block schedule science teachers discover the need to shift from the traditional lecture-and-discussion approach to instruction and toward a more hands-on, project-oriented approach. The hands-on, project-oriented approach provides for a more meaningful interpretation of worthwhile objectives of science curricula.

Teaching science in the block allows teachers to design and facilitate learning activities for students that are participatory and inquiry oriented. Experiments, laboratory exercises and investigations, outdoor learning activities, field trips, and cooperative group activities all tend to require flexible time periods that may extend beyond an hour in duration. In the block, teachers are not required to set up and clean up for five or six student groups per day as might be required for active student participation in traditional schedules. If managed properly, class sessions on block schedules allow sufficient time to (1) organize material and equipment needed for the learning activities, (2) allow students to explore and seek answers to problems and questions by using concrete materials and making observations, (3) organize data and results, and (4) collect materials and clean up. In some cases, there will be time for sharing and discussion of results and conclusions among individual students and student groups while the information is most timely and relevant.

Many educators believe that students' learning and retention directly relate to the level of involvement of the students in the learning process and the immediate use the students make of the information. Shorter, traditional class schedules do not usually allow the flexibility to enable students to be as actively engaged in the learning activities as they may be when longer blocks of time are available.

A physical science teacher in the block can use activities such as the one in Figure 1.1 (p. 7) as student discovery-type activities rather than as show-and-tell activities to help the students develop and retain desired concepts and skills.

CHALLENGES OF TEACHING SCIENCE IN THE BLOCK

Teaching science in the block affords teachers more flexibility in getting the job done. In most cases, science teachers will have time to begin laboratory preparations and introductory activities, allow students to engage in experiments and investigations, bring closure to the activities and investigations, and supervise clean-up activities within a single class session. There are some challenges, however, that may be heightened when teaching science in the block. Those challenges concern the amount and depth of the content coverage, the management of student behaviors and activities, motivating and keeping all students properly engaged in learning throughout class sessions, and accommodating the student diversity encountered in classroom groups.

DECIDING WHAT TO TEACH

Teachers determine what they are expected to teach by examining the local curriculum guidelines and other materials, including textbooks. They also become familiar with state and national reports and guidelines such as the *National Science Education Standards* (National Research Council, 1996) to determine what and how others think science should be taught. Science facts and information are being generated at such a pace that it is not practical for any individual to retain more than a small fraction of them. Therefore, the suggestion usually is to identify the concepts that are thought to be more beneficial and lasting for students at the present and in the future and concentrate on getting students to learn those concepts well. Broad concepts and themes have been suggested for that purpose. Examples of such themes are:

- The *process of change* as it might relate to life cycles, weather systems, and chemical and physical changes
- The *interrelationships of things in the environment* (among living things and between living and nonliving things)
- *Matter and energy* as they act on each other and are redistributed in the physical and biological environment

While there is no general agreement on exactly what the important concepts of science are, educators do agree that learning a few lasting concepts is more beneficial than memorizing large volumes of easily forgotten facts. If, due to state and local requirements and guidelines, there are specific concepts and information that must be covered, the teacher may have to deviate from the broad themes and concepts suggestion. However, once the required specifics are addressed, the suggested strategy for deciding on content coverage is the same—identify a few important concepts and teach them well. The amount of information covered and the depth of coverage are usually functions of the abilities of the students and the rate at which they learn. It is important to enable the slower students to work through activities and form concepts at a slower pace than faster students. At the same time, all students, even the faster and more capable students, should be challenged to do and learn all that they can.

SEQUENCING THE CONTENT AND LEARNING ACTIVITIES

Science instruction in the block, whether on a four-by-four plan, an alternate day plan, or some other scheduling plan, should be organized to lead the students through the content in a way that facilitates maximum learning and retention. While effectiveness and efficiency are prime considerations in instruction, the developmental levels, learning styles, interests, and other characteristics of the students must be a part of those considerations. Natural resources and conditions and the availability of other resources are also factors to consider in deciding on the sequence of components in a science course. For example, biology teachers may find it desirable and more effective to teach ecology units either early in the fall or late in the spring of the school year when outdoor learning activities can be easily implemented.

FIGURE 1.1 SAMPLE ACTIVITY: FOCAL LENGTHS OF LENSES

Objectives:

After the lesson, the student will be able to:

1. Describe the focal length of a convex lens

2. Indicate what affects the focal length

3. Recognize useful applications of information concerning lenses and their effects on light

Materials (enough for each group of two to four students):

Convex lenses of different thickness

Candles and lighter or matches

Candle holders or jar tops

Meter sticks

White cardboard or construction paper

Small grooved blocks or modeling clay to hold lenses upright

Activities:

(Darken the room.) Ask students to position one of the lenses between the lighted candle and the white cardboard at varying distances until the image of the lighted candle appears sharp on the cardboard. Allow the students to do the same thing with the other lenses of varying thickness. Ask them to measure and compare the distances between the objects (candle and lens and cardboard and candle) for the different lenses.

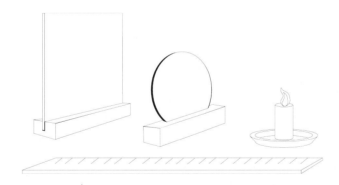

Students should be able to discover the relationship between the thickness of the lenses and the distances between the objects. They should be encouraged to prepare a data table for recording their measurements during the activity. They should discover that the image of the candle on the cardboard is inverted and they may be able to develop an explanation for the upside-down image.

At some point, the teacher may wish to introduce the term *focal length* and the equation used to calculate focal length:

$$\frac{1}{\text{Focal length}} = \frac{1}{\substack{\text{Distance of object} \\ \text{(candle)}}} + \frac{1}{\text{Distance of image}}$$

One of the culminating activities may be to ask students to brainstorm or list applications for knowledge of the effects of convex lenses on light.

When planning a sequence for the content to be covered during a course, science teachers in block schedules may find it helpful to use the calendar for the semester or school year. The school or school district curriculum guide, adopted textbooks, and curriculum map, if one has been developed for the course, will also be helpful. If a curriculum map has been developed, the sequencing task for the teacher may be relatively simple, depending upon the details provided by the map. The map may indicate the topics and units to be covered during particular months and weeks of the school year. There may be flexibility for individual teacher options concerning the arrangement and length of the learning activities, as well as the instructional methodologies employed within a unit or time period. A curriculum guide may serve similar purposes as the curriculum map and may also provide specific information about content coverage and the sequence of that coverage. On the other hand, a guide may be very general and provide considerable flexibility for teachers in sequencing the content and learning activities during a given period of time.

Figure 1.2 depicts an example of a chemistry course sequence chart for a six-week period in a four-by-four block schedule covering three units of content.

When considering single lessons and learning activities, sequencing is usually based on the teacher's philosophy and beliefs about how students learn and the most effective ways to promote learning and retention. Science teachers in block schedules should become well versed in the various instructional models and the results of research on teaching science. They should then apply that information in sequencing and planning learning activities for students in science.

DESIGNING AND FOCUSING THE LEARNING ACTIVITIES

The methods employed for teaching science on block schedules should be those that produce the maximum amount of learning and retention for students. Highly effective science teachers use more student-centered approaches to instruction than other science teachers use. These teachers relate science content to the tools and practices of scientists, to current and relevant conditions and events, and to the impact of science on the individual and on society (see Figure 1.3, p. 10).

FIGURE 1.2 CHEMISTRY SEQUENCE CHART

Chemistry		Days				
Week	Unit	M	T	W	Th	F
1	Physical & Chemical Changes	Phases of matter (observe examples)	Charles's Law & Boyle's Law (show film)	Phase changes (demos)	Chemical properties of substances	Changes in chemical properties
2	Classes of Matter	1. Assessment Activity 2. How we classify matter	Elements and atoms	Chemical symbols and properties	Compounds & representing them	Mixtures and their properties
3		Solutions and identifying them	Identifying compounds & mixtures (lab)	Chemical formulas (examples)	Chemical reactions and what affects them (lab)	Chemical reactions and equations
4	Particles of Matter	Assessments exercises for previous unit	Molar relationships (lab)	Gases and gas laws	Applying gas laws	Atoms and subatomic particles
5		The periodic chart	Grouping the elements	Chemical bonding and molecules	1. Assessment activities 2. Shapes of molecules	Factors affecting reaction rates
6		Energy of chemical reactions		Acids and bases	Properties of acids and bases	Assessments activities and intro to new unit

---

Figure 1.3 Instructional Approaches

Teacher-Centered ◄——————► *Student-Centered*

Lecture	Student Experimentation
Discussion	Interactive Media
Demonstration	Problem Solving

Generally, the more the learning activities engage students and the more senses the students employ during the learning activities, the greater the students' (1) depth of understanding, (2) ability to apply the concepts and skills, and (3) retention of the concepts over time.

Teacher-centered lessons and student-centered lessons can include the same concepts or content. Science teachers, however, must make decisions about whether to design the learning activities so students become major participants in the activities or listeners and viewers as the teacher performs. The decisions should be based on the value of the activities to students and the resources available. For example, in the water density activity described next, a teacher can exercise options in structuring the lesson. First, the teacher can decide to describe what should happen and why it is expected to happen, given certain conditions (give a lecture). Second, the teacher can prepare the materials, manipulate the materials, describe to students what is done, and explain the results as the students observe (do a demonstration). Either of these teacher-centered approaches will require less time and materials than allowing students to cover the same concepts by experimentation or other student-centered methods. The student-centered approaches, however, may be more valuable to students in terms of depth of learning and retention. The longer class sessions in block schedules are conducive to employing student-centered approaches because of time flexibility. Figure 1.4 shows a sample lesson with the activities provided involving a more student-centered approach than would a lecture or a teacher demonstration including similar content.

Figure 1.5 (p. 12) reveals the relative value of having students engage in various participatory actions during science lessons. The more senses and skills (listening, seeing, touching, doing, etc.) the students apply during the learning process, the greater is the potential for deep understanding and for retention of concepts learned.

FIGURE 1.4 A STUDENT-CENTERED LESSON DESIGN

How Temperature Affects Water Density

Question to pose to students:
How does temperature affect the density of water?

Hypothesizing:
Ask students to form in groups of 3–4 and brainstorm to develop a response. For example, students may eventually make a statement such as: As temperature increases, the density of the water decreases. This will become the hypothesis statement. Then, ask students to suggest ways to test their answers.

Ask students to develop a plan for investigating or testing their hypothesis, given the following materials: a *large pan or container for water, cold water, warm water or heating source, small flask or bottle for warm water, food coloring.* The teacher may wish to provide some direction and assistance here. Strategic questioning may be used to help the students think critically and develop a viable plan.

Plan for the investigation:
Instruct students to put cold water (may use ice) in the pan. In the bottle or flask place hot but not boiling water. Add a few drops of food coloring to the water in the flask or bottle. Cover the opening of the flask or bottle and submerge it into the pan of cold water. Then, remove the cover. *The students should observe and record their observations as the water at the two different temperatures meet.*

Analyze the data:
Students should analyze the observations. They may also draw some inferences based on the observations. Ask the students what the movements of the water reveal about density. Then, ask them how the results of the investigation relate to their hypothesis. Do they support or refute their original hypothesis?

Conclusions:
Students should develop a concluding statement based on the hypothesis tested. Questions for consideration may include: Are there any other phenomena in nature that we can relate to the results of the investigation? Are there other implications of the results? What would happen if the initial locations of the warm water and the cold water were switched? What are some extensions to the investigation that could be pursued?

FIGURE 1.5 HIERARCHY OF STUDENT ACTIONS FOR LEARNING

Learn information and use it to instruct others.
Teach the information.

Practice using the information.
Apply it in new ways.

Discuss it with others.
Talk about the information.

Observe a demonstration.

Observe an audiovisual presentation.

Read the information.

Hear a lecture.

Direction of Learner Involvement
for Increasing Retention Rate

MOTIVATING STUDENTS TO PARTICIPATE IN SCIENCE

Not all students come to the classroom enthusiastic about participating in the science learning activities. Science teachers have a responsibility to identify or design and present learning activities in a manner that encourages and motivates student involvement and learning. Fort (1993, 675) writes of children in America being born into science-shy homes in science-shy communities and attending science-shy schools where science-shy approaches to instruction (lectures and textbooks) are used. Science teachers must recognize students who come from homes and communities where participation in science study and science activities are not considered appropriate and accessible for everyone. For those students, extra effort is required to change their attitudes concerning science study and its relevancy to their lives.

Science teachers often worry about how to get students interested in the content of the lessons and units they teach. In particular, student motivation is a concern for teachers planning to teach in a block schedule. Students who are not motivated, but are restless for the extended periods of time, can cause behavior problems as well as limit their abilities to learn the information intended. Effective teachers try to get and maintain students' interest because they know that if the students are motivated to focus their attention on the content of the lesson or unit, then providing experiences to help them learn will be relatively easy. Getting students to wonder or inquire about the content of the lesson, if only in their own thinking, is the first step to helping them to learn the new information or to meet the objectives of the lesson. Motivation derived from curiosity will lead students to seek answers and get involved in lesson activities. Developing introductory activities to boost students' curiosity is used successfully by many science teachers. Once their curiosity reaches a certain level, students become anxious for answers and closure.

Science teachers on block schedules are encouraged to develop and implement strategies for determining students' interests, goals, and concerns. Teachers may talk to students and parents or use other means, including short questionnaires, to discover information about students' backgrounds, experiences, aspirations, and interests. Brief questionnaires can be developed and administered prior to teaching a unit to determine what types of content, examples, and activities might be of most interest to the students in a class. For example, before teaching an earth science unit on the weather and climate, the short survey questionnaire in Figure 1.6 could be administered.

FIGURE 1.6 INTEREST SURVEY QUESTIONNAIRE

Name: _____	Date: _____

Choose an answer for each statement below that is closest to what you know about yourself. Your responses will not affect your grade.

Statement About You	*Circle Your Answer*
I often wonder about why there are different types of clouds.	Agree Not Sure Disagree
I listen to or watch the weather report often.	Agree Not Sure Disagree
I would prefer to live where the climate is warm most of the time.	Agree Not Sure Disagree
I am not usually interested in the weather.	Agree Not Sure Disagree
I think experiencing changes in the seasons each year is better than having one type of climate all year long.	Agree Not Sure Disagree
I do not think the weather affects people very much unless there is a major change like a hurricane, tornado, or blizzard.	Agree Not Sure Disagree
I think studying about the weather and climate will be fun.	Agree Not Sure Disagree
I already know a lot about the weather and climates.	Agree Not Sure Disagree
I want to learn more about how scientists predict the weather.	Agree Not Sure Disagree
I want to know why the weather is different in the different seasons of the year.	Agree Not Sure Disagree

When possible, science teachers should choose learning activities that are meaningful or relevant to students by drawing on current community events and concerns to initiate and maintain student interest. To maintain interest, students must experience some degree of success and accomplishment.

A learning environment should be maintained that motivates students to want to learn. The students' concepts of themselves, especially in relation to science and the topics covered, can affect their motivation. The science-shy students, those who believe they have low aptitudes for learning science, and those who cannot envision themselves participating in science in the future, are not likely to be motivated to study science. Therefore, teachers have a responsibility to get to know their students and make efforts to help all students understand how science is relevant to them and why it is important for them to learn science. In addition to the individual progress students may be able to discern for themselves, they will respond positively to the positive feedback and encouragement they receive from their teachers. Hassard (1992, 55) states that feedback is critical to the development of knowledge.

Providing options and giving students opportunities for input into aspects of the decision making related to the class activities can be motivational for the students. Therefore, giving them opportunities to help plan some class activities and make decisions will be highly motivational for the students to participate in the learning activities and meet lesson objectives.

THE SCIENCE CURRICULUM AND LONG-TERM PLANNING FOR THE BLOCK SCHEDULE

When people get ready to accomplish something that is important to them, they spend a significant amount of time planning for it, and are influenced by what they value and what actions they deem important to ensure reaching their goal. Teaching and accomplishing certain goals and results from the teaching effort should invoke a similar motivation to plan. Without extensive planning, teachers have difficulty providing effective instruction on photosynthesis, genetics, plate tectonics, or magnetism. Teaching requires planning and purpose. It helps if teachers begin with the most incipient question: What is my mission? Or, what are the desired outcomes? If teachers can envision the "ideal product" and plan to make the outcome possible, they can be successful regardless of the scheduling plan. A statement attributed to Vince Lombardi is, "If you don't know what the end result is going to look like, you can't get there from here." The statement is appropriate for teaching science.

PLANNING TO MEET GOALS

Planning is very important to effective teaching regardless of the scheduling format used. In a block schedule, all of the curriculum personnel, including teachers, need to effectively plan in order to meet the desired objectives and take full advantage of the instructional time and resources available. Because class sessions are fewer but longer, it is important to plan and implement the instruction to avoid wasting valuable time. This is not to imply that every minute of time has to be structured. If, however, explicit learning objectives are not identified and strategies are not planned for accomplishing the objectives and determining when they have been met, there is great risk that the instruction will be ineffective.

Going to block scheduling can be deceiving because teachers tend to focus on having 90 to 110 minutes instead of the typical 45 to 50 minutes for a class session. They sometimes forget that more time per class session also means fewer class sessions. The overall instructional time will not be greater. What the teachers once included in two sessions, they must now try to do in one longer session. However, dividing the class sessions into parts, following the same pattern, and using the same lessons that were used on the old schedule will not work and may not be pedagogically sound. On a four-by-four block schedule where more and longer class sessions are scheduled within a week and semester, more varied and engaging learning activities for students are desired. Ninety-minute lectures will not suffice in any case. Students who were able to force themselves to sit through 45-minute lectures on polyatomic ions will not be attentive, and may not be well-behaved, during longer lectures.

Science teachers in a block schedule should resist the temptation to lecture and use other expository approaches to instruction for long periods. They should plan to include more cooperative learning activities and those that allow students to physically manipulate materials. Audio-visuals and other devices may also be helpful for altering the modes of instruction and facilitating the learning and reinforcement of concepts. Care must be exercised, however, to cover the content needed to accomplish course objectives. Many teachers who experience teaching in the block for the first time get over halfway through the semester or year and discover that they have covered less than half of the content intended. This can be devastating. Therefore, careful planning and management of time is essential, especially early in the process.

One strategy is to begin with local and state-level objectives and guidelines (if they exist) for the course or subject. In some cases, end-of-course competency tests are adopted or required by the state. In those cases, the alignment of the course content and the science curriculum to include the content of the tests is obviously an important consideration for teachers. The alignment of the curriculum with the requirements of objectives and assessments will help to ensure some level of accountability. Teachers who fail to respond to the requirements, regardless of the merits of their other accomplishments, usually do not experience pleasant results.

Science teachers should consider identifying and outlining the units or general topics they deem important for the subjects taught. This activity may be done by all of the science teachers in the school or district. Working in groups to accomplish the task will increase individual confidence and support as well as appropriate connections among the courses and grade levels. Initially, the content topics or categories should be as broad as possible. Then, the individual teacher or teacher groups can establish pacing guides to ensure adequate coverage of the content or each subject, relative to scope and depth, during the semester. Listed in Figure 1.7 are the content topics that may be used for a biology course.

FIGURE 1.7 BIOLOGY COURSE TOPICS

Content Units	Content Areas
1	Chemical Basis of Life
2	Cellular Biology
3	Genetics and Evolution
4	Classification and Diversity of Organisms
5	Ecology
6	Human Anatomy and Physiology

Using the six broad topics listed above, the teachers should identify the important unit components (topics, lessons, and activities) associated with each. A good textbook can provide ideas of where to start, but the final product should be based on referring to and drawing from more sources than a single textbook.

An actual topic outline given to students taking Honors Biology is shown in Figure 1.8, with a breakdown of units and the approximate number of class sessions allotted to each topic. This outline was used in an A/B, odd-even, block schedule with 110-minute classes meeting every other day of a school year.

Providing appropriate time and depth for each topic area is a difficult task in long-term planning. This will require several years of trial to perfect, and the process is continuous. To further develop the curriculum, teachers should adjust the topic areas into a logical order to ensure content progression and the building of a knowledge base. For example, they may not wish to cover speciation without first covering the principles of genetics, which should be preceded by the study of nucleic acids.

Other factors that influence the sequence of topics in a science course may relate to the seasons of the year and when resources are available locally. For example, in some geographical areas, a unit on plants may be best taught in the spring or fall rather than in the winter months. Equipment sharing among teachers in different classrooms or buildings, the need and availability of consumables, and, sometimes, standardized testing schedules all may affect when topics are taught.

FIGURE 1.8 HONORS BIOLOGY TOPIC OUTLINE

Six-Week Period	Unit	Lesson Topic	Number of Class Sessions
1	Chemical Basis of Life		
		Chemistry Introduction and Review	2
		Biochemistry/Organic Compounds	5
2	Cellular Biology		
		Structure of a Cell	4
		Cell Division & Reproduction	3
		Reproduction and Development	3
3	Genetics and Evolution		
		Mendalian Principles	3
		Applied Genetics	5
		Biotechnology	4
		How Populations Evolve	3
		Origin of Life and early Earth Conditions	2
4	Classification and Diversity of Organisms		
		Taxonomy	2
		Viruses	2
		Monerans	1
		Protozans	2
		Fungi	2
		Botany	5
		Zoology	6
5	Ecology		
		Biomes	2
		Population Ecology	4
		Community Ecology	4
		Ecosystem Ecology	3
6	Human Anatomy and Physiology		
		Integumentary System	2
		Nervous System	3
		Musculoskeletal System	3
		Digestive System	3
		Endocrine System	2
		Circulatory-Immune System	4
		Respiratory System	3
		Excretory System	1
		Reproductive System	2
			80

CURRICULUM MAPPING AND SCIENCE IN THE BLOCK

School personnel have a tendency to either follow curriculum guides in a rigid and lock-step manner or develop and follow guidelines that are so loose and vague that no one is sure who should be doing what at what time. Teachers need to have a macro (district level) view of curricula, as well as a micro (classroom level) view. A curriculum map is a device that provides teachers with a clear picture of what they should teach in a specific grade and in a particular discipline to form a comprehensive curriculum. A curriculum map will indicate how the curriculum of a particular grade level and discipline fits into and relates to the curricula at other school levels and in other subjects. (Jacobs, 1997, 3–4)

Curriculum mapping is a systematic process of developing a description of content taught, when it is taught, and the amount of time spent teaching it. Teachers may be asked to complete logs on a daily basis to indicate what they taught and how much time was devoted to it. The resulting product provides a picture of how much time is spent on instructing students concerning specific concepts, skills, objectives, or behaviors. Comparisons, therefore, can be made between the course content desired and that which is actually taught. The curriculum mapping process "is based on the concept that the quantity of time teachers allocate to a learning task has an effect on student achievement, and that curriculum decisions should be based on accurate information, not opinions" (Clough, James, & Witcher, 1996, 79).

Curriculum mapping may be valuable for science teachers adjusting to block scheduling to make sure they are taking full advantage of the instructional time available. The process of mapping, as well as the resulting maps, will assist teachers and their supervisors to analyze the curriculum they implement and make adjustments to better meet the instructional objectives they identify. Curriculum maps may include:

- The amount of teacher time on task
- The scope and sequence of the curriculum
- The percentage of time allocated to a topic
- Information showing whether there is duplication of content taught in the curriculum
- The alignment of curriculum taught with objectives and assessments
- Agreement between actual curriculum and curriculum guides, textbooks, etc. (Cough, James, & Witcher, 1996, 80).

Clough, James, & Witcher (1996) emphasize that curriculum mapping should not be considered as a replacement for daily lesson planning by teachers. They also state that curriculum mapping should not be used to evaluate teachers. They indicate, however, that the following information can be obtained concerning teacher performance.

- Course content actually taught.
- Instructional activities used with students
- Curriculum modifications made for students with special needs
- Teaching strategies employed
- Textbooks and/or supplemental materials utilized
- How often the skills tested by achievement tests are taught

Multilevel and across-level planning and communication are required to create curriculum maps that (1) reflect the macro view of curriculum and (2) will be used by science teachers for instructional planning at the classroom level. In other words, developing curriculum maps that will be used effectively depends on cooperation and communication among the instructional and supervisory personnel within a school or school district. Teachers should not teach science concepts and skills in a vacuum, but they should know how the planned instructional content relates to other components of the curriculum that come before, at the same time, or after the instruction they will provide. Jacobs (1997, p. 5) states that "Curriculum mapping amplifies the possibilities for long-range planning, short-term preparation, and clear communication." Curriculum coordinators or curriculum supervisors in school districts may be expected to provide leadership and coordination for developing broad district-wide curriculum maps. Curriculum mapping requires involvement from teachers and curriculum decision makers (Clough, James, & Witcher, 1996).

Jacobs (1997) suggests the following steps for effective curriculum mapping:

- Each teacher completes a calendar-based curriculum map reflecting what he or she actually taught—providing authentic data in real time.

- Each teacher reads through the maps developed by the other teachers in the discipline, department, and/or building and checks for repetition, gaps, meaningful assessments, matches with standards, and potential areas for integration and timeliness.

- Mixed groups of teachers (from the different disciplines and grade levels) read through the maps to locate gaps, repetitions, potential areas of integration, mismatches between outcomes and curriculum, and meaningful or nonmeaningful assessment.

- All teachers meet to receive a report on the findings of the prior activities and to decide whether the remaining work should be done in the large group or smaller instructional units—teams.

- Based on the observations made, faculty members, teams, and/or administrators determine the areas that need to be addressed and revised immediately (or in the short term).

- Curriculum groups and teachers decide on issues and components of the maps that will require long-term research and development.

♦ All those involved will continue the review cycle periodically and frequently taking advantage of the available technology to help make the process easy and effective.

RESOURCE UNITS

Many teachers find it beneficial to develop resource units for the topics and discipline components they teach. A resource unit is a collection of a wide variety of activities and materials that can be used to teach a particular topic. It is designed as a flexible reservoir of resources from which the teacher can select activities and materials to provide a unit of instruction for a specific group of students at a given time. From the resource unit the teacher should be able to develop a specific teaching unit for one or more groups of students by considering their unique interests and abilities. The teacher should also be able to use the resource unit to plan and provide instruction for class sessions of different lengths (scheduling blocks).

The teacher needs to develop an effective storage and filing system in order to be able to retrieve the resources when desired. Separate file folders or containers for each topic may facilitate organization and retrieval of the materials. A computer filing system may also assist with planning, organization, and retrieval.

TEACHING/INSTRUCTIONAL UNITS

The teaching unit is developed with a specific group of students in mind while also considering the learning environment and the length of the instructional sessions. If the teacher already has a resource unit or units related to the topic or theme of the teaching unit, it will be a matter of selecting the materials to provide appropriate instruction for the student group. Deciding how to organize or sequence the learning activities to best utilize the available resources, including time, for teaching the students will also be an issue. Using a variety of instructional approaches and building on the knowledge and skills students already possess are important. These factors become even more critical to the effective use of time when teaching science in a block schedule. The teaching unit will usually include the following:

♦ Unit title

♦ Descriptive statements and relevant information about the students and how the unit should be implemented to accommodate their abilities, interests, etc.

♦ The unit objectives (learning outcomes desired)

♦ Materials and equipment needed (including reference sources and computer software)

♦ Instructional activities (the learning activities that the students are expected to participate in during the unit)

- Timetable (approximate times to be allotted to each activity and the entire unit)
- Assessments (evaluation plan, tests, and other assessment instruments and activities, and the relative weights to be assigned to each activity and/or product)

2

SHORT-TERM PLANNING: DEVELOPING LESSONS AND LEARNING ACTIVITIES FOR SCIENCE IN THE BLOCK

THE VALUE OF PLANNING

Teachers make hundreds of decisions each day while instructing and supervising students. Many of these decisions must be made instantaneously and without significant thought, research, or discussion. With ample short-term planning, teachers can alleviate some of the stress of trying to make impromptu decisions. Prior thought and planning concerning actions and anticipated student reactions tend to serve teachers well and enable them to feel confident and in control.

Changing from a traditional schedule with 50-minute class sessions to 90- to 110-minute block sessions can be stressful and reduce teaching effectiveness if preparation and prior planning have not occurred. Successful teaching in block sessions requires more than clumping two traditional sessions together. It requires new approaches to instruction and varying activities during a class session to maintain student interest, as well as to cover the intended content in the time allotted.

In a block schedule, it becomes even more critical to get students actually involved in their own learning and to keep them on task during the available time. Otherwise, a semester will pass, and less of the content will be covered than is intended. It takes careful and deliberate planning to stay on task and to provide stimulating and meaningful learning experiences for students. Effective teachers realize the importance of planning lessons that are motivational and meaningful for students at the beginning of the class session, require active student involvement in the middle, and promote reflection and learning at the end.

Wise and Okey (1983) bring out the importance of wise planning by emphasizing four aspects of a well-planned lesson: objectives, feedback, use of materials, and varied activities. They also make the connection between planning and effective teaching by stating:

> The effective science classroom appears to be one in which students are kept aware of instructional objectives and receive feedback on their progress toward these objectives. Students get opportunities to physically interact with instructional materials and engage in varied kinds of activities. Alteration of instructional material or classroom procedure has occurred where it is thought that the change might be related to increased impact. The teacher bases a portion of the verbal interactions that occur on some plan, such as the cognitive level or positioning of questions asked during a lesson. The effective science classroom reflects considerable planning (Wise and Okey, 1983, 434).

DEVELOPING AND USING PACING GUIDES

If you are new at teaching in the block, it may be difficult to determine, on a day-to-day basis, the pace at which you must proceed through a unit of content to be able to cover other important units and topics that should be covered. Using a pacing guide or some other format to plan ahead and schedule activities will be helpful. It is important to remember to focus on teaching a few things well, rather than covering everything in a text or other source about a topic. It is also important to plan learning activities that are student-centered and require the active participation of students, even though such activities may require more of the available instruction time.

Figure 2.1 is an example of a pacing guide an earth science teacher developed and used for a six-week period during the school year. It shows a 30-day (6-week) instructional period, where each row represents a week (5 instructional sessions) and each cell represents a day or class session in a four-by-four block schedule. The *topics* section indicates what will be taught, the *themes* section shows the larger units of content and the instructional sessions they will cut across, and the *methods and materials* section indicates the teaching and learning activities that will be implemented. The titles in parentheses in the *themes* section are catchy titles similar to those some teachers like to use to help motivate students.

FIGURE 2.1 EARTH SCIENCE PACING GUIDE FOR A SIX-WEEK PERIOD

	Day 1	Day 2	Day 3	Day 4	Day 5
Week	**Topics**				
1	What drives the rock cycle: Intro. to plate tectonics	Continental Drift: The earliest evidence	Density Lab	Density, convection, & the inner earth	Plate boundaries
2	Plate boundaries	Types & examples of mountains	Volcanoes: how they form	Why are some volcanoes so violent?	Volcanoes and people: Destroyers or providers
3	Earthquakes & where they occur	Locating earthquakes	Unit Test	Erosion & weathering: Driven by water cycle	Overland flow: Physical weathering
4	Chemical Weathering	Differential weathering lab	Stream systems: watersheds	Streams & evolution	Sedimentation
5	Streams as Transporters	Groundwater Zones	Karst Topography	Living Karst	Unit Test
6	Soil definition & kinds based on formation	Soil cores & profiles	An up-close look at soil components	Chemical components: N,P,K	Greenhouse lab
Week	**Themes**				
1	The constantly changing, dynamic Earth (Moving and Shifting) ⟶				
2	⟶		Volcanoes & earthquakes: Energy from within the Earth (shaking and baking)		
3	⟶		**Unit Test**	Weathering & erosion (wear and tear)	
4	Recycling & building (going through ups and downs)			The role of water (the change agent)	
5	⟶		The Earth's surface shapes and forms (nips and tugs)	**Unit Test**	
6	Earth soils and the life connection (the dirt of life) ⟶				

(Figure continues on next page.)

Week	Methods and Activities				
1	Discussion & lecture: Tectonic theory—inner earth	CD-ROM & discussion	Calculating density of rock type (lab)	Convection models with smoke, water, etc.	CD-ROM on plates
2	CD-ROM & discussion	Hyperstudio stack & discussion	Hyperstudio stack: Hawaii calculation	Modeling continental & oceanic volcanoes	Discussion & video
3	Volcano activity on energy and pressure	Epicenter location assignment & discussion	Unit Test	Group activity: Components of water cycle	Outdoor activity: Finding physical weathering
4	Rock dissolving activity & reports	Differential weathering lab	Mapping activity: Topo maps & stream orders	Hyperstudio pictures	Discussion: deltas, sand bars, beaches; Tom Brown essay
5	TDS lab: Headwaters versus mouth	Groundwater model & activity	Fieldtrip & article—sinkholes, etc.	Performance quiz on mapping & models	Unit Test
6	Discussion: Residual, colluvial, alluvial	Activity: Coring & core analysis	Demonstration: Porosity, permeability, etc.	Lecture: Leaching	Lab: Soil testing in greenhouse

Another approach to developing a pacing guide is to:

1. Determine the total number of days available to teach the science course or a component of the course.

2. Identify the themes, units, and/or topics that must be covered. Use state and/or local curriculum guidelines and objectives to help with this task.

3. Decide how many days can be devoted to each theme, unit, or topic based on importance, content scope, depth of coverage desired, methods of instruction, or the learning activities to be included, etc. Adjustments can be made as the pacing guide is developed and finalized. Figure 2.2 is an example of this type of pacing guide.

**FIGURE 2.2 BIOLOGY PACING GUIDE FOR
30 INSTRUCTIONAL DAYS (6 WEEKS)**

Theme/Unit	Topic	Days	Objective(s)	Methods/Activities
Cells: Units of Life	What is a cell?	1	1, 2	Discussion, Lab 1
	Plants and Animals	1	2, 4, 6	
	Nucleus & Organelles	2	1, 2, 6	Model building
				Assessment/test
Cell Reproduction	DNA, the Molecule	2	1, 2	Model building
	DNA Replication	1	1, 2, 4	DNA isolation lab
	The Cell Cycle	2	1, 2, 4, 6	Discussion
	Cell Reproduction	1	1, 2, 4, 6	Cell survey lab
	Mitosis and Cytokinesis	2	1, 2, 4, 6	Cell division lab (onion & whitefish slides)
	Meiosis	2	4, 6	
		1		Assessment/test
Genetics	Mendelian Genetics	3	1–4, 6, 7	Discussion & phenotype demonstration
	Applied genetics	2	6, 7	Problem solving (monohybrid & dihybrid crosses)
	Biotechnology	2	6, 7	Biotechnology demo (gel electrophoresis)
	Population genetics	2	4, 6, 7	Discussion—genetic disorders
		1		Share research papers on genetics topics
		1		Assessment/test
Organism Reproduction & Development	Asexual & sexual reproduction	2	4, 6, 7, 8	Discussion, film, and diagrams
	Gametogenesis	1	1, 2, 3, 4, 7, 8	Models
	Embryonic development	1	1, 3, 5, 6, 7, 8	Film/video
		1		Assessment/test

Note that assessment appears in the guide in several places with an entire class session designated in each instance. A class session is designated, but rarely should a particular assessment activity last a full 90-minute session. Especially in the case of pencil-and-paper tests, 45 to 50 minutes is the maximum amount of time students should be expected to perform at one time. Teachers can design other assessments that complement or supplement the pencil-and-paper tests if they are given and if the entire class session is allocated to assessments. In some cases, teachers may wish to allot a sufficient amount of time for the assessment activity at the beginning of the class session and use the last 30 to 50 minutes to introduce the next lesson or topic. The assessments may last the entire class session for performance assessments where students are actively engaged in tasks that enable the teachers to discern the students' abilities to apply knowledge and demonstrate skills.

CONCEPT MAPS

Science teachers may find it helpful to use concept maps as planning tools (Figure 2.3). Concept maps can assist in determining an appropriate sequence or hierarchy for the development of concepts within a unit or broad area of study. The maps should be designed to show relationships among the different concepts that may be addressed during a unit of study in science. The visual illustrations make concept maps valuable tools for some teachers as they attempt to decide what concepts are important to include in the lessons. The decisions should be made based on the prescribed curriculum, the developmental levels and interests of the students, and the relevant connections among the concepts. The visual depictions of the concepts and their interrelationships provide teachers and students with roadmaps for the unit of content. The concrete representations tend to facilitate learning and retention for students.

The following steps for developing concept maps in science were adapted from those suggested by Dorough and Rye (1997, 37–38).

1. Identify all of the concepts believed to be important to the topic of study and list them.

2. Group the concepts that are most similar according to content and rank them according to how general or specific they are.

3. Write the central topic at the top of the page and begin linking the concepts by lines with the general concepts near the top.

4. Finish mapping all of the concepts and add additional concepts where appropriate. When linking long strings of concepts, try to place them horizontally rather than vertically.

5. Cross-link concepts in different vertical segments of the map to integrate the map as a cohesive whole.

6. Mark or identify those concepts that are most appropriate for the students.

FIGURE 2.3 EXAMPLE OF A CONCEPT MAP

Climate and Weather Factors

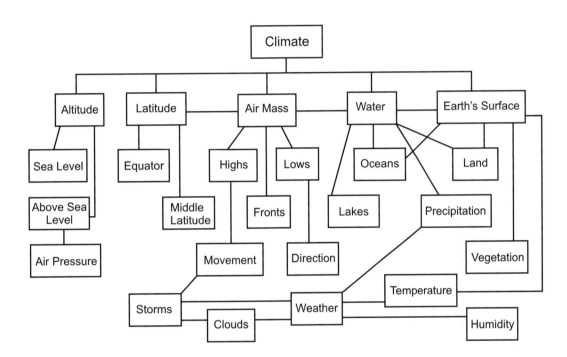

THE LESSON DESIGN

There are a number of ways to think about and structure lesson plans for science instruction in the block. Canady and Rettig (1995) identified a general way to think about a lesson plan that involved breaking the plan down into three components: explanation, application, and synthesis.

Canady and Rettig (1996, 24) borrowed from the work of Phyllis R. Hotchkiss to suggest a structure similar to the one shown in Figure 2.4 for structuring lessons for the block schedule and for keeping students active.

FIGURE 2.4 LESSON DESIGN FOR THE BLOCK SCHEDULE

- ◆ Homework, Review, and Lesson Connecting Activities (10–15 minutes)
  - Individual and group reports of results
  - Brainstorming sessions
  - A game or simulation using previous information
  - Advanced organizer activity
- ◆ Presentation (20–25 minutes) and/or Main Learning Activity (30–35 minutes) (50–60 Minutes Total)*
  - Presentation
  - Videotape
  - Videodisk
  - Student or teacher report
  - Socratic seminar
  - Interactive lecture
  - Activity
  - Lab experiment or investigation
  - Case study
  - Campus field trip
  - Demonstration and observation
  - Learning center
- ◆ Guided Practice and Application (10–15 minutes)
  - Short games
  - Individual and group problem solving
- ◆ Reteach—Actions to Reinforce Concepts and Skills or Correct Misconceptions (10–15 minutes)
- ◆ Closure (5–10 minutes)

* The presentation and learning activity are listed together for science rather than separately, as Canady and Rettig illustrated, because the two components of the lesson can be reversed or merged. Students can still be engaged throughout the time depending on the level of inquiry and the nature of the presentations and activities.

Madeline Hunter (1982) developed and proposed a model for planning and providing instruction that she called the "essential elements" of instruction. It includes:

- ◆ Selecting objectives that are appropriate for the students
- ◆ Teaching to the objectives

- Monitoring students' progress toward obtaining the objectives and adjusting instruction based on the feedback
- Using the seven "Principles of Learning":
    1. Using anticipatory sets to help students make connections between prior knowledge and learning needed to attain new objectives
    2. Using motivational strategies and behaviors to keep students focused and interested
    3. Keeping students actively involved in the lesson
    4. Using reinforcement and the concept that actions and behaviors have consequences
    5. Using "closure" activities at appropriate times during the lesson to reinforce and help students organize what they have processed for learning
    6. Using the principles of "retention" through association with other learning, providing memory cues, modeling, and practice to help students remember the information
    7. Using the principles of "transfer" through application to new situations, contrasting prior knowledge to the new, practicing and testing applications of the "critical attributes" of the new concepts

THE LESSON PLAN

Figure 2.5 shows a lesson plan format that will assist science teachers to develop effective plans. The format will require teachers to think about:
- What is important for students to learn
- What learning activities can be provided to best facilitate the desired learning outcomes
- What instructional materials and equipment are needed
- How to assess the performance and progress that students make toward meeting the learning targets in valid ways

Depending on the type of block scheduling (4/4 semester, alternate-day schedule, or variations of these), the content or unit of study, and the developmental levels of students in class, the feasibility of covering all the components outlined in Figure 2.5 in one lesson may vary. It is important to remember that regardless of the way class sessions are scheduled, variety in activities and proper pacing are the spices that help to flavor the lessons for students.

FIGURE 2.5 A LESSON PLAN FORMAT
---

1. **Identification Items:**

   Teacher's Name: _____ Date: _____
   Class Session: _____ Time: _____
   Theme/Unit: _____ Topic: _____

2. **Key Concepts, Skills and/or Behaviors:**

   Identify one or more main ideas/concepts to be developed. Identify any important skills and behaviors students are to develop or demonstrate as a result of participating in the lesson.

3. **Objectives**

   a. *General Objective(s):* List general statements identifying student knowledge, skills, and attitudes to be developed.

   b. *Instructional objective(s):* Provide specific statements identifying measurable student behaviors/outcomes that will indicate student development of the intended concepts skills, etc. at the end of the lesson.

4. **Learning/Teaching Activities and Time Estimates:**

   Specify the learning activities that will be provided and those in which students are expected to participate. After each activity, indicate the estimated amount of time to be spent on the activity. Do not forget to include formative assessment and closure activities where appropriate. Homework assignments or other special assignments should be included to be certain they are not forgotten and that ample time is allotted to make sure students understand them and have the background information needed to complete them. Include any activities or conditions that will be needed for students with special needs and abilities. Extension and optional activities to the required activities may also be listed.

   a. Introduction and connecting activities (allotted time)

   b. Lesson development and main learning activities (allotted time)

   c. Closure and conclusion activities (allotted time)

   d. Assignments, extensions, and future connections (allotted time)

5. **Content to be Covered:**

   Outline the important content or information to be covered during the lesson. If specific directions and key questions are planned to facilitate discussion, progress, closure, etc., write those directions and questions down.

   a. Key points of the lesson

   b. Key questions to pose

6. Materials and Equipment:

List any materials, equipment, or supplies needed to implement the learning activities beyond those commonly possessed by students attending the class. Include the sources and locations of the items needed.

7. Student Assessment Activities and Tasks:

Identify plans and procedures for checking student comprehension or skill development concerning the lesson objectives. Questions, items, tasks, observational checklists, etc. to use in assessing attainment of the objectives should be identified for use at some point during or after the lesson.

8. Lesson Assessment:

Provide some space for making notations and statements concerning your assessment of the lesson and lesson components. Indicate adjustments or changes that should be made the next time the lesson plan is implemented. Provide reflective statements concerning what should be done differently.

Teachers should check their lesson plans (see Figure 2.6, pp. 34–37) to determine if they provide for the following:

- ◆ Connections to previous lessons
- ◆ Relevancy information and advanced organizers
- ◆ Clear outcomes (objectives) for students
- ◆ Developmentally appropriate learning activities
- ◆ Materials and equipment needed
- ◆ Checking for student understanding during the lesson
- ◆ Assessing student progress on the objectives after the lesson
- ◆ Homework assignments and follow-up activities if appropriate

Making connection to previously learned (covered) content and providing advanced organizers allows students to ask questions and respond in ways that enable teachers to make corrections and adjustments in the students' thinking and understandings. Teachers can make judgments about student reactions to determine where to begin the learning activities of the day or to determine if prerequisite skills and concepts are needed. Using advanced organizers helps students to learn and retain the information for later use. They may also be motivational for the students.

(Text continues on page 38.)

FIGURE 2.6 A SAMPLE SCIENCE LESSON PLAN

Teacher's Name: Ms. Astronia Novice   **Date:** October 9, 2000
Class Session: Earth/Space Science, Even Day
Time: 10:05–11:50 a.m.
Topic: Altitudes of Objects

Concepts or Key Points:

1. The altitude above the horizon of an object in space (as viewed from a particular position) can be measured and communicated.

2. A *degree* can be described as a unit (360th) part of the circumference of a circle.

3. *Altitude* may be defined as the height (or angular distance) of an object above the horizon or above sea level.

4. Observing, measuring, comparing, and interpreting and applying data and information are important science skills (processes).

General Objective(s):

The student will be able to understand how the location of objects in space can be identified and communicated.

Measurable Objective(s):

After participating in the lesson, the student will be able to:

1. Use an altitude finder to determine how high an object is above the horizon.

2. Describe how the degrees of a circle or portion of a circle (arc) can be used to determine the distance of one object from another.

3. Apply the terms horizon, degree, and altitude appropriately in communicating about objects in space.

4. Determine the angular distance of an object from another object or position.

Learning Teaching Activities and Time Estimates:

1. To introduce the topic, pose a question and tell the students that we will be constructing astrolabes or altitude finders. Tell them why the lesson is included (See the beginning of the Content section. (10 min.)

2. Assign the students to small groups, distribute the necessary materials, and give the students directions for building an altitude finder. (See the direction below) (10 min.)

3. Allow time for constructing the instruments. (20 min.)

4. Clean up left over materials. (5 min.)

5. Take students outside to use the altitude finders. Have them take pencil and paper to record the altitudes of different objects. (20 min.)

6. Return to classroom. (5 min.)

7. Identify a student from each group to take the altitude finder home and use it in the evening to determine the altitude of the moon or another object at a specified time after the sun has set. (5 min.)

8. Assign home activities and reading material for the next lesson. (5 min.)

   (Note: the time for the lesson would probably require two traditional class sessions.)

Content to be Covered:

Tell the students that they will be building an instrument that has been used for many centuries since it was invented by the ancient Greeks to determine how far the planets and stars are above the horizon. The instrument, called and astrolabe, was later perfected and used as a navigational tool. The sextant, a more accurate instrument with a small telescope and mirrors, was later developed and used for the same purpose.

Question: How could you communicate the location of a particular star or other object to a friend across town by telephone?

A circle is composed of 360°, so we can use the degree as a unit to communicate location or direction from a reference point.

Materials and Equipment:

For each student or student group

Piece of cardboard 20 × 20 cm (about 8 × 8 inches)

Piece of string at least 25 cm long

Small weight such as a washer or nut

Protractor

Tape

Soda straw

Straight edge or ruler

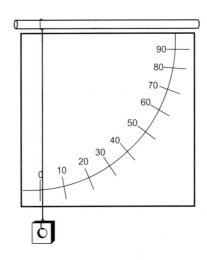

Student Assessment Activities and Tasks:

Observation—Ask each student to determine the altitude of an object using an altitude finder, observe the student in the process and check the results obtained. (Objective # 1)

Pencil and paper constructed response item–Describe how you could use a protractor (and the degrees of a circle) to communicate to a classmate, who is standing with you, where a rock outcropping is from a particular tree that is easy to see. (Objective # 2)

Check the student's activity report to determine if the words horizon, degree and altitude are used appropriately. (Objective #3)

Student tasks—Estimate the distance of the top of a tall building or tree above the ground in degrees. Then, use your protractor or altitude finder to measure the distance. Write both answers down and compare them.

Directions for the Activity—After distributing the materials

1. Show the students that the protractor scale can be used to measure angles from 0 degrees to 180°.

2. Have students place a 0° mark at the lower left-hand corner of the cardboard. Have them place a 90° mark at the upper right-hand corner.

3. Have the students use the length of string (shorter than 20 cm) as a compass to guide a pencil across an arc from the lower left-hand corner to the upper right-hand corner.

4. Now have the students divide the arc they formed by marking 10 intervals from 0° to 90°—that is, 0°, 10°, 20°,..., 90°. The protractor can be used to help mark the divisions.

5. The students should now tie the nut or washer to the string and tape the free end of the string to the upper left-hand corner of the altitude finder. The string should cross the 0° mark when the upper edge of the cardboard is held horizontally.

6. The soda straw should be taped along the upper edge of the cardboard to be used as a sighting device. Tell the students that they will be sighting objects through the straw, along the top of the cardboard, with the string on the edge of the cardboard that is farthest away from them.

7. When the students have constructed their altitude finders, take them outside to find the number of degrees that such things as chimneys, treetops, or lampposts are above the horizon. Be sure they do not try to sight the sun with their altitude finders because it may damage their eyes.

8. Encourage the students to "take turns" taking their altitude finders home to measure the number of degrees visible object such as the moon and certain stars are above the horizon.

Key Questions

1. Why do you think we attached a weight to the string? (To pull the string straight down.)

2. Sometimes people use the term *angle of elevation* when they use an astrolabe. What do you think the term means? (How many degrees the object is above the horizon.)

3. Does the altitude finder tell you anything about the direction the object is from you? (No.)

4. How could you find the direction? (Use a directional compass.) (Note: The next lesson and activity in the unit requires the students to make an instrument that can be used to measure the angle of an object from true north.)

Extension

The students may be asked to use the library or the Internet to research the use of the sextant in modern sea navigation. They may be able to identify encyclopedias and other sources to find pictures of sextants and diagrams of how they operate.

Assessment of the Lesson

(Example: Need to plan for more time to build the instrument. It might help to cut the cardboard to the required sizes before distributing it to students. The students appeared to enjoy the activities.)

(Other measurable objectives related to the general objective which is part of a unit:

1. Determine the directional location of an object with an azimuth finder and a compass.

2. Locate an object or body in space when given (a) an accurate description of its location relative to the students location and (b) the necessary instruments (compass, altitude finder, and azimuth finder).

3. Indicate that the positions of objects or bodies in space can only be described relative to the locations of other objects, positions, or directions.)

INSTRUCTIONAL OBJECTIVES

In planning and implementing instruction, provisions should be made to ensure the interrelationships and consistency among the three aspects of instructional design. Those three aspects are objectives, instruction, and evaluation as shown in Figure 2.7. The objectives are important, not only for identifying what students are to learn, but (a) to give direction to the instructional methods used and the content to be covered and (b) to give direction to the evaluation process and content. Therefore, a degree of consistency among the objectives, instruction, and evaluation is essential to sound planning and teaching.

FIGURE 2.7 THE INTERRELATED ASPECT OF INSTRUCTIONAL DESIGN

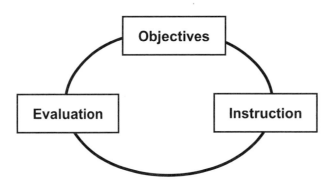

Some educational objectives are stated in broad, general, or long-range terms. Such objectives are often referred to as general objectives or goals. Objective statements that are general or broad are usually open to many interpretations and, therefore, may be operationalized in many different ways. Objectives developed for use at the school district or even at the local school level may consist of general statements of desired instructional outcomes. The individual teacher should be able to use the general statements of objectives to form or identify more specific objective statements for directing the specific learning activities and the assessment strategies planned at the individual classroom level.

The following statements are examples of broad objectives, goals, or learning targets.

   ♦ The ability to properly use science tools and instruments (a descriptive statement).

   ♦ The student will understand that light is a form of energy (a learning target statement).

   ♦ To appreciate instruments used to help predict the weather (an infinitive statement).

While these objectives are considered to be worthwhile objectives, they are general statements that are vague and open to a variety of interpretations by different teachers and students. Given objectives of this type, science teachers may find it worthwhile to develop clear and more specific statements that will directly inform their instruction and enable them to develop valid procedures for assessing students' performance. Then, based on success in meeting the specific objectives, the teachers can make inferences about meeting the general objectives and goals.

When planning for science instruction, if specific, clear, and directly "measurable" objective statements are not provided, science teachers should develop such statements before planning and implementing the instructional and assessment activities. The statements should identify the "student behaviors" expected to result from the instruction or after the student participates in the learning activities. The objective statements should also include overt, rather than covert, behavioral terms. Overt terms such as "state," "identify," "demonstrate," "develop," and "deduce" tend to specify observable student behaviors. Covert terms such as "know," "appreciate," and "understand" indicate student behaviors and conditions that cannot be directly observed and therefore need further specification and delineation. The behaviors identified should be directly observable and/or indirectly detectable (measurable) through the students' acts and products. Consequently, we refer to the statements that identify the desired student behaviors as being measurable objective statements. The behaviors identified should be those that can be demonstrated by the individual student. Examples of measurable instructional objectives are:

♦ The student will be able to *describe* the difference between a mixture and a compound.

♦ At the end of the lesson, the student will be able to *state* the properties of a gas.

♦ The student will be able to *develop a model* to represent the number and relationships of the protons, neutrons, and electrons in an atom of carbon.

♦ The student should be able to *design and perform* a demonstration to show the control of one or more variables.

Note that the behaviors (or action verbs) in the objectives are described in reference to the individual student to imply a focus on each individual student rather than on an average of the performance for the group. Also, the behavior is not described in terms of what the teacher will do, but what *the student will be able to do*. The phrase "at the end of the instruction, the student will be able to" helps teachers to focus on the fact that they should be teaching something the student has not already mastered but will be able to master at the end of the planned instruction. Without that focus, some teachers forget to distinguish between what are primarily teaching/learning activities and what are primarily assessment/evaluative activities. Assessment and evaluative activities should be designed to help determine if the objectives have been accomplished after the relevant instruction has been provided or when the teacher does an assessment. Using the future tense in objective statements also helps teachers determine the most appropriate times to administer the summative or end-of-instruction assessments.

Some authors advocate stating the standard or level of student performance and the conditions under which students are expected to meet the standard, as well as the behavior. The resulting objectives include all three elements—the desired student behavior, the minimum level of acceptable performance, and the conditions under which the student is expected to perform. An example of this type of objective is:

Given pictures of the different types of clouds, the student will be able to label the cloud types with at least 80-percent accuracy.

The first phrase in the statement gives the conditions, and the "80-percent accuracy" phrase describes the minimum level of performance. The inclusion of these phrases in all instructional objectives is not always necessary, especially in those cases where the conditions and acceptable level of performance are implied. Experienced teachers may not find the detailed and extended statements as valuable as novice teachers might. It is important that teachers teaching in block schedules do not come to regard writing good and useful objectives as an exercise in trivial pursuit.

In planning for an instructional unit, science teachers should identify the objectives related to all three of the major domains of learning as identified by Bloom et al. (1956). Teachers should also develope objectives that relate to the development of student abilities at all levels of the three domains. The three domains are:

1. The cognitive domain that consists of the cognitive skill levels, including knowledge, comprehension, application, analysis, synthesis, and evaluation.

2. The psychomotor domain consisting of the skills of moving, manipulating, communicating, and creating. (This category of objectives relates to the development of gross and fine muscle control and includes control of the complex and creative locomotor control involving originality and unique operations.)

3. The affective domain consists of receiving, responding, valuing, organizing, and characterizing. (This domain relates to appreciations, attitudes, and values. Instructional objectives in this domain may require behaviors that can be assessed to make inferences about the skill categories of the domain—they are addressed indirectly or covertly, though others are addressed overtly.)

The idea is for science teachers to keep the taxonomy of educational objectives in mind when they plan lessons. They should remember to help students develop abilities at the upper levels of the domains as well as at the lower levels. If teachers aim at the higher levels of the domains in their objectives and teaching, they will not focus on trivial facts and activities that only require students to follow directions and recipes. Understanding the hierarchical nature of the skill levels of each domain will help science teachers develop objectives that result in higher levels of achievement among students.

Guidelines for writing meaningful and useful instructional objectives include:

- ◆ Think about and jot down the most important things for the students to learn or know, understand, appreciate, and/or be able to do related to the topic.

- ◆ Develop general goals or objective statements from the notes.

- ◆ For each goal or objective statement, develop one or more specific objective statements that provide:
  - The expected student (not teacher) behavior or performance
  - The after-instruction student behavior expected rather than something about the lesson content, the learning process, or the instructional procedures
  - The minimum level of performance and the conditions under which the performance is to occur, if needed

- ◆ Make sure there are sufficient specific objective statements for each general statement to judge when the general objectives have been achieved, based on student performance concerning the related specific objectives.

- ◆ Check to make sure the objectives address all relevant and important aspects of each domain based on Bloom's *Taxonomy* (Bloom et al., 1956).

- ◆ Develop each specific objective to focus on one student outcome rather than on several student behaviors, products, and/or tasks. Objective statements can be clear and concise to provide direction for instruction and assessment without undue emphasis on trivial behaviors associated with the lower categories of the cognitive domain.

THE INSTRUCTIONAL ACTIVITIES

The sequence for the learning activities in science during a class session in the block can be planned and implemented to include an introduction, the main teaching or learning activities, and a conclusion, as shown in Figure 2.8.

Science teachers teaching in the block should use a variety of instructional techniques and approaches to adapt to the topics being taught and accommodate the students based on learning styles, backgrounds, interests, and developmental levels. Most students, however, respond positively to instructional activities that allow them to be active participants in their own learning. Therefore, science teachers should be diligent in their efforts to employ student-centered activities for science instruction.

FIGURE 2.8 RECOMMENDED LESSON COMPONENTS

♦ Introduction/Motivational/Connecting Activities

The introduction should be designed to attract students' attention and motivate them for what is coming next. It may also involve activities or information to make connections between the previous lessons and the information and activities of the learning activities to come. Advanced organizers and set induction activities and information may be considered introductory. Inquiry-oriented and thought-provoking questions are often appropriate to introduce a learning activity.

♦ Teaching/Learning Activity

The instructional activity is designed specifically to help the students achieve the identified lesson objective(s). The purpose of the activity should be to help the students develop the skills, attitudes, understandings, behaviors, etc., for achieving the objective(s) and for continued progress.

Be sure to provide for individual differences when planning and implementing the learning activity. This is especially important if the student group is significantly heterogeneous relative to individual abilities or achievement in the associated content area.

♦ Closure/Conclusion

It is usually very important that a lesson or learning activity has closure or a recognizable conclusion. The conclusion can be in the form of summary comments or activities designed to reinforce the major points of things that should have been gained from the lesson activities. A brief review of the lesson objective(s) and a statement connecting the activity to the students' performance and/or achievement may be in order.

Example That Includes the Three Lesson Parts

♦ Introductory/Motivational/Connecting Activity:

The introduction to a lesson on classification in biology, chemistry, or earth science may involve the teacher distributing familiar and/or common objects to students for them to group or classify before providing them with any other directions. The objects can include leaves, seeds, shells, buttons, or a combination of similarly familiar objects. Students should then be asked to organize the items into three or four groups. Typically, depending on the items distributed, individual students will group the items differently. A brief discussion will reveal that all students have explanations for their groupings. The students may discover that agreement on some basics for grouping the objects will enable them to communicate information about the objects more easily and quickly.

♦ Teaching/Learning Activities:

Include the main concepts of the lesson.

- Biology: The grouping of living things (taxonomy).
- Chemistry: The grouping of elements of the Periodic Chart.
- Earth Science: The classification of rocks and minerals.

♦ Closure/Conclusions:

Review the instructional objectives related to grouping or classification. Discuss how specific classification systems relate to the introductory activity. Ask how classification systems help people in other fields of study and other activities.

As in any classroom situation, it is helpful to get to know your students as soon as possible. Students respond more positively to teachers who learn and use their names when addressing them. There are several effective strategies that teachers can use to learn students' names quickly. They include using seating charts and assigning students to specific seats, taking photographs of students, and jotting down descriptions that the teacher can associate with the names of the students until they are learned. Getting to know about students as individuals also may help science teachers be more effective. Students have different backgrounds, personalities, likes and dislikes, goals, and fears. Awareness of some of these things can provide information that helps teachers to motivate and work with students as individuals. Science teachers can plan learning activities that allow them to interact with students through conversations, discussions, and conferences. The activities facilitate student-centered and individualized approaches to learning. In addition to getting to know their students individually, effective science teachers know the content they teach very well and know how to teach what they teach.

The different teaching methods that science teachers can use in the block in a student-centered way include:

♦ Laboratory and investigative activities (individual and/or small groups) that allow students to pursue the answers to questions and solutions to problems

♦ Inquiry experiments (individual and/or small groups) that require higher-level science process skills

♦ Fact-finding and observational activities (field trips, library search, etc.)

♦ Problem solving (individual and cooperative groups)

♦ Interactive discussions (student to student and student to teacher)

♦ Brainstorming sessions

- ◆ Debate sessions
- ◆ Panel discussions and presentations
- ◆ Simulations (using computers and other devices)
- ◆ Case study activities
- ◆ Projects (if research or developmental)
- ◆ Computers and interactive software activities
- ◆ Games

In general, science teachers should choose the method that facilitates students' involvement in their own learning, but there are times when other criteria need to be considered as well. Those criteria include:

- ◆ What is the best method for students to learn and retain the content in the manner required by the instructional objectives?
- ◆ How long are the students' attention spans during instruction using the different methods?
- ◆ How well are the students able to manipulate abstract ideas mentally?
- ◆ What is the value placed on getting all students to learn the content? Must the content be mastered by everyone?
- ◆ Are the time and resources available to use the best methodology? If, not what is next best?

In determining whether the lessons are teacher-centered or student-centered, science teachers can assess:

- ◆ The ratio of teacher talk to student talk during the class sessions
- ◆ The ratio of teacher-to-student questions, compared to the ratio of student-to-teacher questions, and the ratio of student-to-student questions
- ◆ The percentage of the class session time that students are passively listening to or observing the teacher, compared to the percentage of time the students are actively engaged in doing science (manipulating the materials of science and brainstorming)
- ◆ The percentage of class session time allotted to reading the text or other printed materials or individually responding to those materials.

Figure 2.9 shows a sample instructional activity.

(Text continues on page 47.)

FIGURE 2.9 A SAMPLE INSTRUCTIONAL ACTIVITY

Topic: The Density of Objects

Goal: Understand the concept of density and describe the density of an object in relation to the mass and volume.

Student Objectives:

1. Measure the mass and volume of small objects.

2. Given the measurements for the mass and volume an object, determine its density.

3. Apply knowledge of density to describe why objects float or sink.

Introductory Activity

The teacher can begin a lesson on the relationships among volume, density, and mass by facilitating a discussion concerning the concepts and asking questions to get students to think critically about the ideas. A set of questions might begin with the following: Will all objects that float in seawater also float in fresh water? Why or why not? If an object floats in both seawater and fresh water, will it float at the same level above the surface?

Most students in high school can provide explanations about why objects sink and float in water. All students may not have sound explanations but they have explanations concerning the phenomenon. The teacher may do an introductory activity concerning the relationships among volume, mass, and density as an inquiry demonstration activity to get students interested and motivate.

Materials Needed:

> One or two hard-boiled eggs
>
> Container of table salt
>
> Two large beakers or jars
>
> A large spoon
>
> A large, clean container for water

Procedures:

1. (This step may be completed prior to class time if desired.) Add table salt to enough water in the large container to fill one of the beakers. Add salt until the water is close to saturation level. Allow the salt that does not dissolve to settle out of the liquid. Then, fill one of the beakers about three-fourths full with the salt solution and fill the other beaker to the same level with tap water.

2. With the spoon or your hand, place one hard-boiled egg in each of the beakers. If students are not yet aware that one of the beakers contains a salt solution, the teacher may ask a question concerning why one of the eggs floats and the other sinks. The teacher may proceed with the questioning until the discussion involves references

to the differences in the liquids and, perhaps, to the concept of density, even if the word is not mentioned. The idea of the relationship between the volume and mass of the liquid to the volume and mass of the object is important for students to begin developing.

Learning Activities and Procedures

Materials and Equipment Needed:

Volume measures such as graduate cylinders

Objects and substances for which the volumes and masses can be determined (e.g., blocks of wood, plastic, and metal; sponge; bar of soap; etc.)

Balance and standard masses or other devices for massing objects.

Procedures:

1. Provide groups of students with objects or substances for which they can determine the volumes using measuring devices in the classroom. Then have the students determine the masses of the objects or substances and record the measures.

2. Discuss the objects and the concepts of volume and mass to ascertain the students' understanding.

3. Discuss the meaning of density as the amount of material (matter or mass) in a defined space (volume). Density can be expressed in the following statement or equation:

$$Density\ (D) = \frac{Mass\ (M)}{Volume\ (V)}$$

4. Have the student groups calculate the densities of the objects and/or substances for which they determined the volume and mass earlier. Then, order the objects and substances from most dense to least dense.

5. Have students in groups discuss and decide (hypothesize) which objects/substances will float and which will sink in tap water.

6. Ask students to test the tentative decisions (hypothesis) they made in step 5 and explain or provide a rationale for any hypothesis or tentative decisions that were not acceptable after the tests.

Object or Substance	Volume	Mass	Density	Sink/Float Guess	Test Result
Wood					
Plastic					

Closure Activities

The teacher may wish to return to the discussion and activity involving the boiled eggs to allow students to infer and explain the observations they made. They should also be allowed to ask any questions they have about the activities and receive answers. Can the students explain what density is and express the relationship among density and volume and mass? Can they clearly and correctly explain why objects float or sink in a liquid?

THE ASSESSMENT/EVALUATION PROCEDURES AND ACTIVITIES

Assessment should be a continuous process of receiving feedback based on students' actions and reactions before, during, and after instruction. Teachers make observations, judgments, and decisions concerning student learning and performances throughout an instructional session. In many cases, teachers adapt their instruction based on the feedback from students. The more forethought and planning teachers devote to the assessment process, the more effective they become, not only in doing the assessments, but also in teaching.

The three types of assessments that science teachers need to attend to concerning the content taught are *diagnostic/prescriptive assessments, formative assessments*, and *summative assessments*.

DIAGNOSTIC/PRESCRIPTIVE ASSESSMENTS

Diagnostic/prescriptive assessments are those that precede instruction for a lesson or unit of instruction (see Figure 2.10). These assessments are done to help teachers plan to instruct the students. Assessments done prior to instruction are used to determine if the students possess the prerequisite skills, knowledge, attitudes, and abilities needed to meet lesson objectives effectively and efficiently. Likewise, the assessments are done to determine at what level the students are functioning relative to the objectives or if they have already mastered the content of the objectives and lessons. Teachers may implement the diagnostic assessments in informal ways by asking students questions to review what they know, can do, or think about information related to the objectives and planned instruction. Teachers may also use more formal approaches by administering pretests, surveys, questionnaires, and oral interviews.

**FIGURE 2.10 RELATIONSHIP OF DIAGNOSTIC/
PRESCRIPTIVE ASSESSMENTS TO INSTRUCTION**

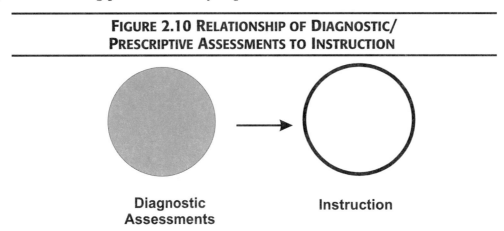

Diagnostic
Assessments

Instruction

FORMATIVE ASSESSMENTS

Formative assessments occur throughout instruction to determine how well students are learning from the instruction (see Figure 2.11). Teachers gather feedback from the students, usually through observations and interactions, to use in modifying the instruction and improving learning. Although teachers may plan and ask specific questions or employ other formal strategies periodically to check for student understanding and progress during the lesson, most teachers also use informal approaches to formative assessments. It is advisable for science teachers in the block to use questioning and other strategies for checking student learning and progress throughout the learning activities. Otherwise, they run the risk of covering large segments of content over longer periods of instruction time before discovering that students are not making progress and able to perform as expected or desired.

FIGURE 2.11 RELATIONSHIP OF FORMATIVE ASSESSMENT TO INSTRUCTION

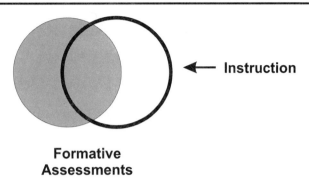

← **Instruction**

**Formative
Assessments**

SUMMATIVE ASSESSMENTS

Summative assessments are those that occur after instruction to determine if the students have learned the information taught and to show how well it has been taught and learned (see Figure 2.12). These are the type assessments that most students and teachers know about and tend to emphasize. Often, summative assessments are focused on determining gains at the lower end of the cognitive domain with little attention to changes and progress toward learning critical process skills and developing appropriate attitudes and values. However, all of the areas of learning should be addressed in summative assessments and other types of assessments, especially if the instructional objectives include them. The cognitive performance levels and gains probably receive greater emphasis during summative assessments because the results of these assessments are used to determine students' grades and to provide achievement reports to students, parents, and others.

FIGURE 2.12 RELATIONSHIP OF SUMMATIVE ASSESSMENTS TO INSTRUCTION

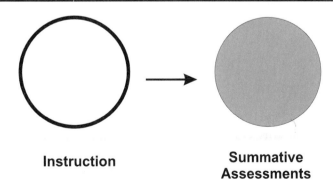

Instruction   **Summative
Assessments**

It should be noted that the types of assessments do not, and perhaps should not, form clear dichotomies. For example, a summative evaluation for one lesson or unit of content may also serve some diagnostic purposes for subsequent lessons. Likewise, summative-type information may be collected during instruction on occasions.

The assessments that should weigh heavily in judging the effectiveness of the lesson and the success that students have experienced are those designed to determine if the instructional objectives have been achieved. Therefore, science teachers should take these assessments seriously and allot enough time to ensure a degree of validity in making instructional and grading decisions. (See Figure 2.13 for an example of an assessment.) A key rule for teachers should be to use the instructional objectives identified for the lesson to guide the development of the assessment instruments, tasks, and procedures. If the objectives of a lesson emphasize the development of process skills, the understanding and application of concepts, and creativity, then the assessments should emphasize those same aspects of learning. Science teachers need to give special attention to the relationships and consistency among the instructional objectives, the teaching-learning activities, and the assessments when planning and implementing instruction. Science teachers should consider the following guidelines for ensuring proper assessments of instructional effectiveness and student progress toward achieving lesson objectives:

1. Write down each objective or a word or number to represent the objective.

2. Identify the best, most feasible method(s) to assess or evaluate each objective.

3. Design the evaluation items, tasks, observations checklist, rating scale, or other devices that correspond with the appropriate assessment method with attention to validity concerns.

4. Check and revise the assessment tools and strategies against (or compared to) the objectives and the facts, concepts, skills, attitudes, and behaviors identified based on their importance and scope.

5. Design the scoring strategies and schemes to be as reliable and fair as possible.

6. Administer the assessments at the appropriate time.

7. Score the assessments.

8. Use the assessment results to determine the appropriateness of the assessment measures and strategies, the effectiveness of the instruction, and the performance of students relative to the objectives.

FIGURE 2.13 SAMPLE STUDENT ASSESSMENT ACTIVITIES

The sample assessment activities presented below are designed to check for student attainment of the objectives identified for the sample lesson in the previous section on page 45. The objectives are:

1. Measure the mass and volume of small objects.

2. Given the measurements for the mass and volume an object, determine its density.

3. Apply knowledge of density to describe why objects float or sink.

Assessment tasks for objectives 1 and 2

Provide several objects that were not used in the teaching/learning activity and request that each student determines the masses, volumes, and densities of the objects. These tasks can be done as center activities if the appropriate materials are provided and the activities can be monitored adequately.

Give each student problems with any two of the three properties (mass, volume, and density) provided and ask that the third property be calculated.

Assessment task for objective 3

Set up a Cartesian diver system and show the students how it operates (how it goes up and down in the liquid). Ask the students to draw a line down the center of a sheet of paper, and ask them to write their observations in the left column as they manipulate the system to get the diver to move up and down in the liquid. Then, ask the students to explain the observations concerning the Cartesian divers, relating cause and effect.

A Cartesian Diver System

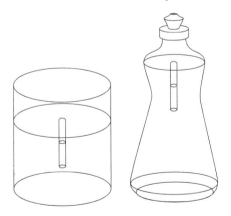

Directions for Setting Up a Cartesian Diver System

Materials (per student group or in assessment center activity):

Large, clear plastic bottle with airtight lid (Clear, empty dish detergent bottle works well.)

Small test tube (1 cm or less in diameter)

Medicine dropper

Large beaker

Water

Procedures:

1. Fill the plastic bottle with water.

2. Fill the beaker with water.

3. Partially fill the small test tube with water, place a finger over it, and invert the tube in the beaker of water. Note how high the tube floats in the beaker. Repeat this step with varying amounts of water in the tube until the bottom of the tube floats just slightly above the surface of the water.

4. Carefully lift the tube vertically and place it gently in the water in the plastic bottle. (You may need to practice this step several times.) The tube should float to barely break the surface of the water as it did in the beaker.

5. With care, a small amount of water may be poured out of the plastic bottle before placing the top on the bottle and making it airtight.

6. Squeeze the sides of the bottle to determine if the tube sinks when pressure is applied and floats when the sides are released.

The chart in Figure 2.14 provides a scheme that science teachers may use to determine how the attainment of each objective might be assessed. Teachers can also check to determine if they are assessing objectives in more than one way to accommodate different students as well as to identify the most appropriate assessment strategies based on the content of the objectives.

FIGURE 2.14 ASSESSMENT DECISIONS BASED ON OBJECTIVES AND PURPOSES

	Test		Task		Observation		Self-Report
Objective	Selected Response	Constructed Response	Product	Action	Checklist	Anecdote	Solicited Response
1	true/false items	short answer					interest inventory
2	multiple-choice & true/false		research paper		oral questions		
3		essay answer	lab report			group co-operation	
4	multiple-choice items		a drawing				
5			portfolio	oral report			
6	matching items		journal	lab demo			attitude survey

3

INSTRUCTIONAL STRATEGIES FOR TEACHING SCIENCE IN BLOCK SCHEDULES

TEACHING STRATEGIES AND METHODS FOR SCIENCE

Some teachers make a conscious effort to implement particular instructional strategies to achieve certain outcomes. Other teachers find themselves implementing certain strategies based on their personalities and beliefs, what is familiar, or what seems to work at a given time, without conscious effort and critical reflection. In other words, some teachers may place emphasis on planning specific strategies and lesson sequences to promote specific types of learning, while others may use specific strategies based on what seems practical and workable at the time. The abilities, interests, and learning styles of the students, along with the nature of the content taught can and should affect the series of teaching strategies and techniques used by teachers. It is likely that teachers who spend time planning and reflecting on the consequences of the teaching strategies they use over time are the more effective teachers.

Block scheduling creates an added dimension for teachers concerning the use of instructional time and choice of instructional strategies that work and complement each other during a class session. Teaching effectively for 90-minute periods or blocks of time presents greater challenges and may requires better planning and management of the instructional activities than teaching during shorter 45- to 60-minute periods. The longer class sessions and reduced number of sessions necessitates employing strategies for maintaining student attention and motivation, accommodating different learning styles, and keeping all students on task. Research shows that students need to have a refocusing event occur every 20 to 30 minutes to maximize instructional effectiveness.

Block schedules also increase the need for variety in the instructional strategies. Planning for two or three deliberate changes in activities and refocusing student attention during a class session can be a significant challenge for some teachers.

STUDENT-CENTERED VERSUS TEACHER-CENTERED STRATEGIES

Research has indicated that student-centered science instruction tends to have more long-term value than direct, teacher-centered instruction. The instructional strategies and methods employed by science teachers probably cover the entire range between direct instruction, teacher-centered approaches, and student-centered approaches in which the student takes an active role in the learning activities and may exercise some control over the nature and direction of the activities. All science teachers are expected to make appropriate decisions to provide the most effective instruction for their students based on the resources at hand.

In teacher-centered instruction, the teacher controls the learning activity as information flows from the teacher to the students. The control may be in a direct manner through strategies such as lecture and questioning, or the control may be indirect through strategies such as simulations, concept mapping, and modeling. When using the latter strategies, the teacher may set up the situations but would not control the activity directly. Gunter, Estes, and Schwab (1995) identified six steps in the direct instructional approach:

1. Review previously learned material.

2. State the objectives for the lesson.

3. Present the new material (or learning activities).

4. Provide guided practice with corrective feedback.

5. Assign independent practice.

6. Review both during and at the end of the lesson.

Direct teaching approaches can be used effectively for science instruction in the block, especially to complement and serve as bridges between other approaches and lessons. Indirect approaches, however, are more essential for helping students to develop science process skills and other skills that provide important long-term benefits.

Student-centered instructional strategies allow students to have more active and self-guided roles in the learning process and activities in direct and indirect ways. Based on recent reports, science teachers should provide student-centered and interactive instructional strategies when feasible. In interactive instruction, students interact with one another, the information, and the learning materials. The teacher is more of an organizer and facilitator. During independent learning activities, students interact with the information and materials more than with the teacher or other classmates.

Figure 3.1 provides some assistance for distinguishing between student-centered and teacher-centered instructional strategies. The manner in which the strategies are implemented during the instruction, however, is essential to deciding whether a learning activity is student-centered or teacher-centered and whether the teacher and student roles are direct or indirect.

QUESTIONING STRATEGIES

Teachers ask questions in many different classroom situations, and they ask questions to serve a variety of purposes. Obviously, questions may be asked to invite responses from students in many different contexts but teachers tend to use questions to:

- Determine what the student knows about something
- Determine the student's line of thinking
- Provide directions for the student
- Manage behavior or get the student's attention
- Help the student solve a problem
- Give information
- Encourage discussion

Questioning is a very important instructional tool for the science teacher, especially in teaching in a block schedule. When used properly, questioning can promote student-centered and student-directed learning. Questioning is important for facilitating the lessons and a variety of activities in which students should participate during class sessions in the block. In particular, appropriate questioning strategies are valuable for promoting open discussion, exploration, and experimentation in situations where science instruction is inquiry-oriented, student-centered, or constructivist-based. The science teacher may wish to employ questioning to focus students for the study of a topic, to help students formulate research questions and strategies, to direct student activities, and to help students arrive at solutions. The teacher may also use questions to bring closure to activities and to help students to transition from one activity to another during a class session. Developing skills in the use of questioning to direct student activity and to facilitate transitioning from one activity to another during class sessions in the block is very valuable for science teachers.

Science teachers should encourage students to ask questions of the teacher and other students. The teachers should try to create an atmosphere where students feel comfortable asking questions and sharing information. A classroom environment in which students freely ask and answer questions promotes cooperation and collaboration and enhances learning. One way to promote student questioning is to have students write down any questions they have about the topics covered during a class session and schedule time to address those questions at the beginning of the following class sessions. It may be erroneous to assume that all students are "on board," or attentive, and understand every-

FIGURE 3.1 TYPES OF INSTRUCTION

Classification	Teacher-Centered	Student-Centered	Interactive	Independent (Student)
Direct	• Lecture • Teacher-led discussion • Teacher demonstration	• Student experiment • Student report • Student project	• Brainstorming • Cooperative groups • Socratic seminar	• Research • Independent reading
Indirect	• Simulation • Learning center • Concept mapping	• Investigation • Field trip • Reading assignment	• Game	• Puzzles • Projects • Independent study

Description of a Teacher-Centered Activity

The teacher lectures about the behavior of light when it is reflected by a surface and shows a diagram that depicts the way light is reflected. The teacher points out that the angle of incidence of the light striking the surface will be equal to the angle of reflection if the reflecting surface is smooth. Indirectly, the teacher may structure a learning center where students read the directions and information for themselves or view a video tape on the reflection of light and respond to a set of questions concerning the content of the activity.

Description of a Student-Centered Activity

The teacher brings several tennis balls and/or basketballs to class and asks students to stand at different distances from a partner and bounce a ball so it can be caught by the partner standing and without moving from the designated spot. The teacher introduces the angle of incidence by asking the students, "At what angle (of incidence) must the ball be bounced to have it get to the partner on one bounce? How do you determine how (at what angle) to bounce the ball?" (*The angle [of reflection] at which the ball bounces to the partner depends on the angle at which it was thrown [angle of incidence].*) After discussion, students can be asked to relate the experiences with the ball to the behavior of light when it is reflected and to design a demonstration or experiment to show support for their position or hypothesis.

Materials:

Tennis balls

Light sources

Mirrors

Small paper boxes

Student Activities:

Students should have opportunities to interact and cooperate during the lesson as they depend on each other in teams and as they brainstorm and discuss the relationship between the behavior of the bouncing ball and the light rays. The students may also cooperate and discuss plans to test their ideas and hypothesis about the reflection of light.

Students may be independently motivated to read and seek information in other ways concerning the behavior of light as it strikes a surface.

---

thing that was covered during a 90- or 120-minute period. Addressing the questions presented by students will help them to fill in the gaps.

Among the classroom methods and activities that are compatible for teacher and student questions are:

- Discussions
- Demonstrations
- Media and multimedia presentations
- Student investigations and/or experiments
- Field trips
- Group activities
- Projects
- Games and simulations
- Lectures
- Evaluations and assessments

Science teachers should use questioning wisely to promote the types of learning and learning environment desired. Asking many questions in short periods of time implies the use of convergent questions, which focus on recall or factual information, rather than the use of divergent questions, which require high-level thinking and the application of learned information. Divergent questions are considered beneficial for helping students develop inquiry skills and for promoting an inquiry-oriented and exciting learning environment for the scheduled blocks of time. An example of a convergent (or recall) question is, "How many planets are in the solar system?" An example of a divergent question (or a question at the opposite end of the spectrum) is, "What do you think would be different on the earth if none of the planets in the solar system had a moon?" Figure 3.2 shows the distinction between the two types of questions.

FIGURE 3.2 DICHOTOMY OF QUESTION TYPES

To ask appropriate questions designed to serve the purposes intended, science teachers may need to formulate questions to be asked ahead of time. Designing good questions should be a part of the overall planning for the lessons and units to be implemented. Teachers may wish to review sources such as those by Trowbridge et al (2000, 91–104) and Kubiszyn and Borich (2000, 46–80) that address the domains of learning as well as the types of questions teachers need to ask to cover all levels of the cognitive domain, including the higher levels.

If science teachers are interested in promoting inquiry and open discussion by the students, then they will ask more divergent questions and encourage their students to ask questions of each other and teachers. To encourage inquiry and discussion, teachers must also avoid using a rapid-fire approach to asking questions. Over time, researchers have determined that teachers' approaches to using questions will directly affect the classroom behaviors as well as student learning. Research results indicated that teachers, on average, waited about one second for students to respond to their questions before commenting or going on to ask another student. Again, this approach to questioning implies an expectation of recalled or factual responses rather than responses requiring higher levels of thinking (Tobin and Capie, 1981).

Research has revealed that when teachers increased the wait time (the time students have to respond to the questions), students' responses and classroom behaviors changed significantly. When teachers increased wait time to 3–5 seconds, on average, the following changes occurred:

- Student responses increased in length and sophistication and were more varied.
- Students asked more questions of the teacher and one another.
- Students exhibited more speculative thinking and contributed more inferences.
- Students, even the lower-achieving students, showed more confidence.
- Teachers showed more flexibility in accepting responses.
- Teachers asked higher-level questions and expected higher levels of performance from all students. (Tobin and Capie, 1981, 5–6)

Research shows that benefits are also realized when teachers wait several seconds after students respond to questions before reacting to the responses. The teachers have time to form appropriate reactions, other students have an opportunity to think and respond, and discussion and open classroom participation is facilitated. All students in the classroom are more likely to be involved in the discussions and learn from their participation in the classroom activities.

During field trips, demonstrations, and investigations, the science teacher should be aware of the types of questions asked and the mental operations required by the students to answer them (see Figure 3.3). The "what" questions (those beginning with "what") may be those designed to get responses about student observations. These questions tend to be easier to answer. The "how" questions may require responses concerning procedures or explanations of a happening and may involve making inferences. The "when" and "where" questions concern responding about time and place. The "why" questions tend to require explanations that demand higher-level mental operations. The teacher can plan the order of questions based on the complexity of the answers required to get the results desired. The teacher can ask the questions in order of increasing complexity (based on appropriate responses) to help students learn to approach problems in a logical sequence of steps or operations. The teacher may also wish to make sure different students have opportunities to answer the different types of questions over a period of time.

Remember that all of the questions asked should be followed by pauses (wait times) that are long enough for the students to form appropriate responses. The questioning should be done to make sure the students understand and to keep them actively involved in the activity. The teacher should distribute the questions among the students to facilitate the involvement of all of the students.

GROUP AND COOPERATIVE LEARNING

Science teachers often group students to complete learning activities. Grouping and assigning roles to students are good ways to promote cooperative learning, which will facilitate some important learning outcomes. Students learn to work together to solve problems and accomplish tasks in more natural ways than if competing on an individual basis. Teachers may organize students in a number of different ways for group work and instructional activities that are cooperative in nature. Regardless of the grouping scheme used, science teachers should group students to facilitate their learning and overall development (see Figure 3.4, p. 63).

(Text continues on page 65.)

FIGURE 3.3 USING QUESTIONING IN AN
INQUIRY-BASED ACTIVITY: AN EXAMPLE

This activity can be used as a demonstration to teach gas laws or atmospheric pressure. It works well as a teacher-led inquiry demonstration if the teacher poses questions in a thoughtful manner. Note: The teacher's questions and instructions are in *italics*.

Materials: Empty soft drink cans, hot plate, room temperature water, tongs

Key Question: How does the temperature effect the volume of a gas?

Ask students to respond to this question based on what they know already. One approach is to ask the students to record their answers (or guesses) on paper. Ask them to explain or support their answers. Assure students that they will not be penalized if they cannot give "the correct" answer. The important thing is that they provide a reason for their answers.

Example of a good answer: As temperature increases, the volume of a gas increases.

Show students the materials (soft drink can, hot plate, etc.) you have brought for the demonstration. Then state that you intend to heat a small amount of water in the soft drink can until it begins to boil. Ask the students, *What will happen if I invert the can with the boiling water in the container of cool water?* Their responses can serve as their hypotheses concerning the exercise. Allow students to write down their responses (guesses) or to provide oral responses. You may want the students to give reasons or support for their answers.

At this point, you may question students about the process they just completed by asking, *What step in the scientific or research process did you just complete?* Allow time for the students to formulate their hypotheses. It is often important that students review current research (notes, textbook, etc.) to help in formulating a reasonable hypothesis.

The next step is to have the students develop an investigative plan or strategy. *What should be done next or what is the next logical step to determining if we can accept or reject your guesses?* The questioning should direct the students to plan (or make suggestions) for testing their hypotheses. The teacher can again describe what will be done with the materials and began the activity by alerting the students to *Observe the process closely and record what you observe. List the observations in the order they occur.*

The Demonstration

Place approximately 10 ml of water in the empty soft drink can. Place the can on hot plate and heat until the water in the can is boiling. Make sure all students can see the demonstration but caution them to keep away from the hot plate and heated can. Using tongs, quickly invert the can into the container of water. Pause and allow students time to observe and record their observations.

Why did the things happen that you observed? Explain your observations. Feel free to draw inferences and/or conclusions.

Did your observations and explanations support your guess or hypothesis about the demonstration? Do you accept or reject your original guess? Can you resolve or explain any differences between what you expected or guessed and the actual findings during the demonstration? If your guess or hypothesis statement was in agreement with what you observed, can you expand on or develop a better explanation for the phenomenon after the demonstration than you could before the demonstration?

Does this same phenomenon occur in nature? Where and what are the implications?

What are some extensions to this activity that you would want to pursue? How could your findings be useful to industry? What would happen if you varied the temperature of the water in the can and in the basin?

Now, return to your responses (hypotheses) for the key question: *How does the temperature effect the volume of a gas? Revise or adjust your earlier response based on what you have learned.*

FIGURE 3.4 A COOPERATIVE LEARNING INQUIRY-BASED ACTIVITY: AN EXAMPLE

This activity can be used to teach concepts about the nature of science, the scientific method, and/or the rate of chemical reactions. Groups of 3 to 5 students should be presented with the key question such as: *How does the temperature affect the rate of chemical reactions?*

It is important that students review current research (notes, textbook, etc.) related to the topic to help in addressing the question and contribute to the discussions.

Present each group of students with the materials needed to do the inquiry activity.

Materials: glow sticks (used to show chemical reaction), several beakers, thermometers; have ice and a hot plate on hand.

Ask the students to brainstorm to decide how they might use the materials to address the question. A more specific question directed toward the inquiry investigation may also be posed before or after students are asked to respond to the key question of the lesson. The specific question for the activity can be: *How will the temperature affect the rate of the reaction in the glow sticks?*

Once students have reached consensus on the question to be addressed in the investigation and how it can be addressed using the materials available, they should form hypotheses concerning the question. Allow students to decide through their group process how to proceed with making observations and testing the hypotheses.

A Reasonable Plan of Attack for Groups:

1. Formulate question(s) and hypothesis(es).

2. Develop an investigative plan.

    Students will think through how they might test their hypothesis using the given materials. After writing out a proposed plan, the teacher should validate the procedure before the students begin.

3. Do the investigation.

    Students may work at their investigative plan in several ways. Allow for a diversity of plans. Most will include placing glow sticks in beakers containing water at several temperatures. Several minutes are usually enough to affect the rate of chemical reaction within the glow stick. The same glow sticks can be used for different reactions if they are allowed to sit at room temperature for several minutes between tests.

4. Collect data.

    Have students develop a data table suitable for recording the results of their investigation. Again, allow for a variety of models. Students may wish to assign degrees of brightness to the glow sticks for recording purposes. For example, they may use a scale of 1–10: 1 being very little glowing and 10 being the highest amount of light being emitted. Maybe a light meter could be used to assess the brightness, or another method the students may devise.

5. Complete the analysis.

    Students will need to analyze their data to determine if their original hypothesis is supported or not.

6. Develop conclusions.

    Allow the student groups to develop their own conclusions concerning the investigation and concerning the key question of the lesson (activity). An example is: *As temperature increases, the rate of chemical reactions also increases.*

The teacher may wish to follow up the activity with some questions to students to help them reflect on the relevance of the activity beyond the lesson. These questions may include: *What did you use as a control in this activity? Why was it important? What were the dependent and independent variables? How could your findings be useful to industry? At what temperature should glow sticks be stored to extend their usefulness?*

Web sites on cooperative learning

Optimizing National Education (1998): http://www.opnated.org/1cooplrn.htm

Center for the study of classroom processes: http://artsci-ccwin.concordia.ca/education/cscp/Try_1.htm

Some suggestions for cooperative instruction are:

- ◆ Organize students into groups, using criteria based on desired learning outcomes (for the students).
- ◆ Present the students with their task or problem to solve and provide them with enough structure to begin the process, whether it be brainstorming, developing a model, or designing an experiment.
- ◆ Direct students to develop a plan of action or outline of their planned approach before getting deeply into the process.
- ◆ Monitor the groups' progress closely to avoid undue delays and to keep the students on task.
- ◆ Ask questions and provide suggestions to help guide the students in a direction that will be productive and enable them to realize success.
- ◆ If needed, help the students organize divisions of labor (or shared responsibilities) so everyone can contribute and learn, and the same students do not perform the same tasks for each group activity.
- ◆ Evaluate students on their work as individuals and as groups and make sure students understand from the outset how they will be evaluated.

Some benefits of grouping for cooperative learning include:

- ◆ Students deveop social and human-relations skills.
- ◆ Students get opportunities to explore using their leadership, organizational, and other skills.
- ◆ Students may be encouraged to develop their verbal skills.
- ◆ Students learn to participate as members of a group to solve problems and accomplish goals.
- ◆ Students become more aware of their own strengths and weaknesses.
- ◆ Teachers get to know important things about students' personalities that will help in the teaching and learning processes.
- ◆ Students learn the intended concepts and skills in a natural context (or in a lelarning environment) that is less threatening and, therefore, the learning should be more meaningful.

INVESTIGATIONS AND EXPERIMENTS

Block schedules provide great class-session formats for science teachers who wish to use inquiry-based student investigations and experiments as the bases for their instruction. Inquiry-based investigations and experiments tend to require more time to set up equipment, organize student work stations, allow students to work through the activities, and bring closure to the lessons than expository and direct instructional approaches. The inquiry-based approaches, however, are thought to provide more long-term benefits for students.

In many cases, no distinction is made or needs to be made between experiments and investigations and laboratory exercises. Lawson (1995, 22) defines an experiment as a "set of manipulations or specific observations of nature that allow the testing of hypotheses or generalizations." The key ingredients of true experimenting are hypothesizing and testing the hypotheses by controlling and manipulating conditions to determine if one becomes more or less confident in the hypotheses statements (projected conclusions). In science, the term *investigation* is often used to refer to all laboratory exercises and activities, including those that are not considered "true" experiments. Included in the category of investigations may be activities that are either primarily inductive or primarily deductive, rather than both, as is the case with experimentation. Additionally, verification activities may be referred to as investigations. Due to time constraints and the need to meet particular objectives, true experimentation is seldom a reality in the secondary school setting.

Teachers sometimes have students do activities that involve verifying what has been presented. In many cases, students simply follow directions as one would for a cooking recipe. This approach does not allow students to participate in science to the extent advocated by the research on effective teaching of science. Therefore, it should be a lower instructional priority than experimentation. Teachers need to use the science classroom and laboratory to allow students to solve problems and, therefore, construct knowledge of science. The teachers should embrace their role as facilitators in the learning process. Similarly, the students should assume roles as productive learners in problem-solving activities.

Experiments and investigations are the essentials of good science learning. Therefore, it is important that students have opportunities to engage in these activities as individuals and as members of a group. They must be able to function as members of groups and learn to share, negotiate, and help form consensus concerning actions and solutions. Beyond the study of and participation in science, the development of skills in experimenting and doing scientific investigations will help students become effective problem solvers in their other life endeavors.

The belief in cause-and-effect relationships is essential to the learning processes when students engage in inquiry and scientific experimentation. Science teachers, therefore, should take advantage of opportunities to help students clarify and examine their beliefs in this area.

While experimenting, students should learn about and practice the skills of science such as observing, classifying, formulating hypotheses, interpreting data, controlling variables, and defining operationally. Students should learn about what scientists and researchers refer to as:

- Independent variables (manipulated or controlled by the scientist)
- Dependent variables (affected by the treatments or independent variables and studied)
- Constants (unchanged or held constant)

♦ Extraneous variables (may have effects but are not or cannot be controlled)

Students should also learn about the possibility of errors in experimental results and how the chances of those errors can be reduced.

As students progress through science classes, they should be given opportunities to "play" scientists many times. Through the process and practice, students will learn to be open-minded and skeptical to the extent that they will be ready to solve problems and make informed decisions in their everyday lives. The following strategies or steps are suggested for teachers to make certain that some of the learning activities are actually designed as experiments.

1. Indicate whether students are to work as individuals or groups. If they are to work as groups, assign or arrange the groupings.

2. Pose the question or problem students are expected to answer or solve during the investigation/experiment. (Do this prior to beginning the other activities.)

3. Guide students through a brief question-and-discussion period to allow them to guess what the answers or solutions might be (hypothesize). Encourage brainstorming if appropriate.

4. Ask students to develop a plan for testing their hypotheses.

5. Organize the students and classroom space for testing the hypotheses and/or doing the investigative activities.

6. Provide the essential materials and equipment for the students.

7. Coach students in organizing and planning to perform the tests and activities (try out safe possibilities).

8. Question students to make sure they have a reasonable plan of action. They should have a clear idea of the variables of interest and their roles in the experiment.

9. Check to determine if students are ready to record data in an appropriate and retrievable manner.

10. Allow students to set up materials and proceed with activities while you monitor for safety and progress.

11. Encourage students to stay on task and record all of their manipulations, actions, and observed results.

12. When experiments are completed, require that students record their conclusions, especially those related to the hypotheses.

13. Collect, compile, and/or have students share their results and conclusions with the class, depending on the activities and solutions.

14. Compare and discuss the results and conclusions in an inclusive and nonthreatening atmosphere.

15. Remind students to clean up and return materials to their proper places, if desirable.

Teachers can change the order of some of the actions suggested above depending on the topic and the nature of the questions and problems addressed. A class activity is described in Figure 3.5.

DEMONSTRATIONS

A demonstration is a learning exercise or activity in which a phenomenon, concept, or skill is displayed and the physical operations or the manipulation of the relevant materials and objects are done by the teacher, one or more students, or another individual. When a demonstration is performed, the students in the audience are expected to observe and, in most cases, they are allowed to ask questions. The students in the audience may be asked questions during the demonstration to help them understand the purpose of the activity, understand the concepts involved, and draw conclusions.

Demonstrations are usually more effective for helping students to develop important concepts and observational skills than a completely expository teaching technique. For one thing, the students have the opportunity to get more than one of their senses involved in acquiring the necessary information. Investigations and experiments that involve each student in the manipulations and physical operations as well as in the mental operations are believed to be more effective for helping students to develop lasting concepts and important skills. It is easier to keep students motivated if they are involved in interacting with concrete learning materials. During the extended class sessions provided by block schedules, demonstrations can become effective activities and methods for introducing experiments and other activities, helping to transition from one activity to another, and reinforcing or assessing students' understanding of concepts taught using other methods.

Demonstrations may sometimes serve as practical options to allowing students to do experiments and laboratory investigations in science. In making decisions about whether or not to do a demonstration rather than allow students to manipulate science learning materials and equipment, teachers may consider the following conditions:

+ The availability, durability, and cost of the materials and equipment
+ The physical danger involved in letting the students handle the materials and equipment
+ The complexity of the equipment and materials compared to the psychomotor (manipulative) skills of the students
+ The time needed to allow the students to interact with the materials and equipment compared to the benefits or expected results

Justification for doing demonstrations such as "the concepts are too complex and require teacher presentations" can seldom be supported over allowing students to interact with materials and equipment, especially in an inquiry-oriented and student-centered classroom environment. Questions and discussion can be used to promote inquiry during a demonstration (see Figure 3.6, p. 73).

(Text continues on page 75.)

FIGURE 3.5 POPULATION GROWTH ACTIVITY

Goal: Be able to understand what factors affect population size and growth.
Student Objectives:

1. State factors that affect or limit the size of populations.

2. Explain how organism populations grow.

3. Interpret graphs that depict the growth of different populations.

4. Develop a graph or growth curve to represent the change in population density of an organism.

5. Define population sampling and infer from sample data to estimate population sizes and densities.

Materials and Equipment Needed:

Three small jars with lids/tops for each group of students

Microscope

Microscope slides and covers

100 ml graduate cylinder

10% molasses or sucrose (sugar) solution (at least 50 ml per group)

Yeast solution (obtain by thoroughly mixing a cake of baker's yeast in 30 ml of water at room temperature)

Eyedroppers

Learning Activities and procedures:

1. Discuss the definition of population and cite examples.

2. Describe what population density means. Compare the terms *population numbers* (such as number of individual organisms counted) and *population density* (number of organisms within a defined amount of space.

3. Describe population sampling and provide examples.

4. Assign students to groups of 3 or 4 and ask them to identify as many things as they can that affect human populations and population densities. They should explain or provide support for each factor identified.

5. Have the groups exchange the stated factors to determine consensus of opinion. Whole class discussion may be used to resolve differences.

6. Do yeast activity in groups of 5 to 6 students (over 5 days).

   a. State the problem of the activity: How does a yeast population and population density change, and what causes those changes?

   b. Label the jars A, B, and C and place 15 ml of the molasses solution in each.

   c. Stir the yeast solution each time and transfer 10 drops of it to each jar A, B, and C containing the molasses solution.

   d. Using a clean eyedropper, place one drop of the solution from each jar on a clean microscope slide and cover it with a slide cover. View the slide under a microscope on high power (×100). Count and record the number of single yeast cells found. Record the number for each solution in some organized way.

   e. Place the solutions in a warm dark place and follow the same procedure used in step (d) each day for a 15-day period. (If it is impossible to make the counts over weekends, the teacher may allow students to extrapolate the counts for Saturday and Sunday.)

   f. Develop line graphs to represent the population growth in jars A, B, and C. What if the cell counts across the 3 jars are calculated for each day and then plotted on a graph?

7. What conclusions do each group provide? Refer to the problem statements in step 6a.

8. How are the findings and conclusions from the yeast activity related to the ideas and conclusions reached about human populations in steps 2 and 3?

Day	Jar	Cells per Drop	Cells/ml of Solution	Observations and Notes
1	A			
	B			
	C			
2	A			
	B			
	C			
3	A			
	B			
	C			

	A			
4	B			
	C			
	A			
5	B			
	C			

Another variation is to have some groups place varying amounts of molasses solutions in the jars (e.g., A = 10 ml, B = 15 ml, and C = 20 ml) and follow the same procedures.

Student Assessment:

1. List as many factors as you can that affect or limit the size of populations. Then, state how or why each factor affects the size of populations. (Objective #1)

2. Explain how organism populations usually grow when conditions are close to ideal and when limiting factors are introduced into the environment. (Objective #2)

3. Explain the relationship between the changes in the rabbit population and the fox population in a region as depicted on the graph below. (Objective #3)

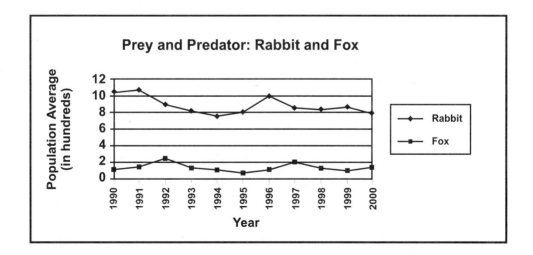

4. Develop a growth curve to represent the changes in the squirrel population in an area based on the data recorded below.

	Year									
	1985	1986	1987	1988	1989	1990	1991	1992	1993	1994
Number of Squirrels	100	114	121	101	88	67	59	63	70	75

5. A school lawn measuring 70 meters by 120 meters is covered with grass of approximately equal types and consistency throughout. A group of biology students choose a spot on the lawn that appears to be representative of the entire lawn and makes a square meter plot at the spot with string and popsicle sticks to form the corners. If the students count carefully and determine that there are 18 clover plants in the square meter area, is it possible for them to estimate the number of clover plants in the entire lawn? If they do generalize (infer) from the sample (plot) to the entire lawn concerning the clover population, what should they determine is the size of the clover population on the lawn? (Objective #5)

6. Define or explain the concept of population sampling. (Objective #5)

7. Explain why scientists might use sampling to estimate populations. (Objective #5)

FIGURE 3.6 AN INQUIRY DEMONSTRATION

Topic: Burning and Physical and Chemical Changes

Goal: To understand that physical and chemical changes occur when something burns.

Possible Student Objectives:

1. Make and report accurate observations.

2. Distinguish between an observation, an inference, and a conclusion.

3. Develop reasonable hypotheses.

4. Develop valid conclusions based on testing hypotheses.

5. Explain what happens when a substance burns.

Materials Needed:

1. Pie pan or shallow dish

2. Short candle with small holder

3. Wide-mouthed jar that the candle holder will fit into

4. Water

5. Food coloring

6. Matches

7. Timing device (watch with second hand)

Learning Activities and Procedures:

The key in this activity is to involve students in the activity through questions and discussion without giving the students specific answers.

1. Question and answer: Ask students what happens when something burns. Let the students volunteer their own answers without assessing who is correct and who is wrong.

2. Light the candle and ask students to explain the phenomenon of the candle continuing to burn. Again, the teacher should ask questions but not dampen inquiry by giving excessive amounts of information.

3. Now, it is time to ask students to guess (hypothesize) what will happen if the wide-mouth jar is inverted over the candle. (They may be asked to write their guesses on paper.) Have the students give reasons for their answers. For students who believe the candle will stop burning, ask them to predict and record how long they think the candle will burn after the jar is placed over it. (Again, have them give reasons.)

4. Ask students to record their actual observations as you demonstrate by placing the jar over the candle.

Guesses & Predictions	Reasons	Actual Observations	Reasons	

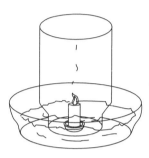

Arrange to have the time recorded from the instant the jar touches the surface under the candle to the time the candle stops burning. Repeat this step several times making sure the air in the jar is allowed to return to the conditions of the air in the room after each observation. (Another variation is to place the jar over the candle again without allowing the conditions to return to normal. Ask students to average the times for each series of trials and to explain (develop a conclusion about what happened).

5. Pour water in the shallow pan to a depth of between 2 and 3 centimeters. Add and stir into the water several drops of the food coloring. Quickly but gently place the lighted candle in the middle of the shallow pan. Repeat the questions and procedures used in steps 3 and 4 above but remind students to observe the jar very closely from their positions.

6. Have students record their observation: What happens to the candle flame (time it stays lighted), to the water in the pan, and to the inside of the jar?

7. Ask the students to infer about what they observed. Ask how they might test their inferences and guesses. Also, ask students what will happen if a mouse is placed in the jar with a burning candle, without the water.

LECTURING

According to science education research reports, science teachers tend to lecture or make verbal presentations more often than they should. Teachers lecture because it allows them to cover large quantities of content in less time than other instructional methods. Lecturing does not require the use of instructional materials and equipment so the preparation time required for lessons is not as extensive as for other methods. To reduce teacher anxiety about time and the scope of coverage, teachers need to be reminded that the emphasis should be placed on learning important concepts, deep understanding essential themes, and knowledge that can be generalized beyond the specific activities, rather than covering numerous facts that students will not retain.

As in any scheduling format, science teachers should use teaching methods and strategies that allow students to be actively involved in discovering and developing concepts and understandings for themselves. There are times, however, when lecturing may be appropriate and indispensable. Lecturing is a method of instruction that can be employed with large groups, allowing more than one class group to be served at a given time.

In block schedules, however, lecturing for science instruction should be kept to a minimum. When teachers or other individuals make exclusively verbal presentations to students in secondary school science classes, the presentations should not last for more than 15 minutes without a break. The break may be used to check for questions and student comprehension or to reinforce the important concepts that were presented through demonstrations and other ways. We suggest that for 90- or 120-minute class sessions, no more than one-third of any class session be allotted to straight teacher talk. Even then, the talk should be in small segments, alternated with other activities that supplement, complement, or reinforce the information contained in the lectures.

When science teachers plan and present lectures they should:

- ◆ Plan the lectures to help students focus on an explicit theme and on the supporting facts and information by presenting them early and in an interesting manner.

- ◆ Provide students with a structure for the information to help them with note taking and comprehension. Develop an outline with space for notes to share with students prior to the lecture.

- ◆ Supplement the verbal presentations with visuals and illustrations when possible.

- ◆ Monitor students to determine if they are alert and comprehending the information.

- ◆ Speak clearly and use terminology students can easily understand.

- ◆ Stay on the topic as planned and do not make unplanned long verbal detours.

- ◆ Summarize key points in the presentation to help students get the essential points of the lecture.

Figure 3.7 provides an example of a 15-minute lecture.

FIGURE 3.7 EXAMPLE OF A LECTURE
EPISODE ON THE SCIENTIFIC METHOD

Introduction of Theme and Purpose

If I ask you to use the *scientific method* today, what would you do? (A rhetorical question.) You may have already used or participated in the use of the scientific method in science classes, and perhaps you have addressed problems and issues in your everyday activities. Beginning today, I want you to be able to communicate about the *scientific method* and apply it in solving problems and discovering knowledge. I want you to be able to describe in your own words:

1. What the scientific method is
2. Its value to scientists and others
3. How knowing about and developing skills in applying the scientific method will benefit you

In other words, the purpose of my presentation is to assist you in learning more about the scientific method, about its importance to scientists and others for learning and discovering new things, and about how you can use the scientific methods to your benefit. *Raise your hand and ask questions at any point during the presentation, especially if you do not understand what I say.*

Information Presentation

You should think of the scientific method as a series of systematic steps or actions that can be taken when seeking answers to questions and solutions to problems. These steps or actions must follow a logical sequence and be based on a belief in cause-effect relationships rather than on superstition and random supernatural occurrences. For example, concluding that a person encountered a problem (had bad luck) because he walked under a ladder two days earlier, when no observable (causal) relationship can be established to connect the two events, is considered superstition rather than science. However, stating an inference or a conclusion based on (1) making observations of people over time as they walk under ladders, (2) determining what happens to those people as they walk under the ladders, and (3) comparing those observations to an equal number of observations of individuals who walk around the ladders involves using aspects of the scientific method. Suppose one observed that 25% of those who walked under the ladders had paint or other objects dropped on their heads, bumped their heads on the ladders, or encountered other problems connected to the act of walking under the ladders. If he observed that during the same period of time a much smaller percentage of those who walked around the ladders encountered the problems, he could at least hypothesize (or make a scientific guess) concerning the issue and the related question. The hypothesis could be further tested.

In employing the scientific method, an individual may wonder about the answer to a question that occurred to him or her after making observations. Based on further observations, the person guesses or speculates about the answer. In other words, he or she forms a tentative hypothesis as in the example concerning the ladder. The person may then be able to predict that given certain conditions, specific things will occur or that specific conditions will cause specific effects (establishing a cause-effect relationship). He or she may also be able to control and manipulate conditions to test his predictions. If the guess about the effect is borne out, then he or she is more confident that the tentative hypothesis offers the answers to the question.

Though the scientific method can be described as containing the steps of (1) defining the question, (2) forming hypotheses, (3) making observations and/or controlling conditions to test the hypothesis, and (4) drawing conclusions, it should not be viewed as a lock-step series of actions as you might have heard before. It provides a general procedure for learning or discovering new things in a systematic way. At any point in the process, the individual may find the need to use another step or to return to the beginning. For example, after beginning to test the initial hypothesis, the individual may decide to stop and define a new hypothesis or revise the initial hypothesis base on the further observations. The scientific method as used by scientists and others is not an infallible and totally objective process. Often, at the end of the series of steps or when the testing of the hypothesis is near an end, more questions develop that can keep the scientist busy indefinitely. Conclusions resulting from using the scientific method can also be wrong, but other methods of learning tend to result in even more errors.

A Possible Visual Aid

```
                    Observations
                    Questions  ─────────────┐
                    Problems                │
                    Ideas                   │
                                            ▼
Synthesis        ┌──────────────┐        Hypothesis
Conclusions      │ A Logical &  │        Theory
Inferences       │ Systematic   │        Prediction
                 │ Process      │
                 └──────────────┘
        ▲                                   │
        │                                   ▼
        └────────── Experiment  ◄───────────┘
                    Collect Data
                    Test
```

As you use the scientific method to discover things, it is desirable to keep an open mind so you will be less likely to rely on false information. If you record your actions and results as you use the scientific method, other people should be able to follow the same steps and methods you followed under the same conditions and repeat the process to verify the results. Otherwise, you may have difficulty getting other people (especially scientists) to believe the results.

Closure (Closing/Summary Statements):

To summarize, the scientific method is an orderly cycle of steps or activities that scientists and others use to help them find the answers to questions and to learn new information. *Are there any questions about what I have said?* (Wait an ample amount of time). *The questions you should be able to answer based on what I stated are:*

1. What is the scientific method?
2. Who uses the scientific method and why?
3. Will the scientific method be of value to you and why or why not?
4. What is an example of a problem or question you might address using the scientific method?

Can you answer those questions? Do you have additional questions for me?

A handout for the students will contain the listed items in the *introduction*, the listed items in the third paragraph of the *information presentation* section, and the list of four questions in the *closure* section. The students may also get a copy of the diagram for reference. The sample presentation will involve using between 900 and 1,000 words and under classroom conditions will usually require 10 to 15 minutes to present, especially if students ask questions or make comments. This is about as long as any classroom lecture should be. Of course, in the block, teachers can present more than one brief lecture during a class session if needed, provided the lectures are separated by other activities such as experiments, brainstorming sessions, and investigation involving student action and participation.

CONCEPT MAPPING

As noted in Chapter 2, page 28, concept maps are diagrams showing what are thought to be meaningful relationships among concepts and propositions (connecting words and descriptions). Concept or cognitive maps are visual maps indicating some of the pathways that may be taken to connect meanings of concepts. Students may be asked to write the names of concepts and their subcategories. Then, they may be directed to draw lines to connect the concepts and subcategories based on the perceived relationships among them. The next step is to have students label the relationships indicated by the connecting lines. A concept map may be more effective if the broader, more inclusive concepts are at the top of the map with the more specific and less inclusive concepts at the bottom of the map so as to depict a hierarchical structure.

Concept maps may enable teachers to facilitate the construction of knowledge by the students. Science teachers may use concept maps to convey to students the *key concepts to be learned* and to reveal *linkages between what the students already know and the new information to be learned*. Dorough and Rye (1997, 37) recommend the use of concepts in science to probe preinstructional understanding, as advanced organizers for lessons, and to evaluate postinstructional knowledge. The authors state that concept maps can be used as study tools and self-assessment tools by students because they allow the students to assess their own understandings. Concept maps may be used to promote cooperative learning if small groups of students are allowed to discuss interpretations and work together to produce group concept maps.

The topics or concepts identified may be discussed as individual parts of a unit of instruction. Based on the discussion and other class activities, students are expected to understand not only the individual topics but also the interrelationships of the topics. The teacher can help students to develop and/or reinforce their understanding of the interrelationships by showing in the mapping diagram how the concepts and topics are related. Students may also be given opportunities as individuals or in small cooperative groups to form concepts maps based on what they have learned. It is important that students provide explanations or reasons why the organization and connections of their maps are provided and structured as drawn. Often students will discover or recognize connections and relationships that the teacher had not discovered.

Students may be asked to identify the concepts to be included in their map, after a general heading and directions for forming the map are given. Another option is to provide the concept words that should be included in the map and direct students to form the map and give reasons for the structure. Figure 3.8 is an example of a concept map.

FIGURE 3.8 EXAMPLE OF A CONCEPT MAP

Understanding the Relationships Among Biosphere Components

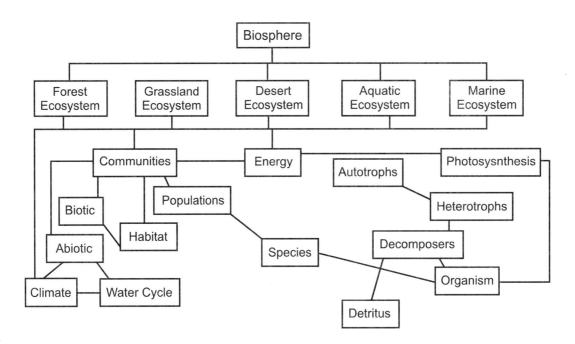

In the map in Figure 3.8, *biosphere* is considered the broad topic or concept of the unit of study. The different types of ecosystems found within the biosphere are connected directly to the biosphere because they form the next level of organization conceptually when considering the system of living things on Earth. The next step is to connect the next largest concepts, showing how they relate to each one of the ecosystems. At certain levels, the connections can be complicated by the desired to show a large number of connections. The idea is to show connections that will show as many interrelationships as possible, while not sacrificing clarity of understanding.

MODEL BUILDING (USING MODELS AND ANALOGIES)

An important goal science teachers should have is to help students develop mental models of the principles and natural phenomena that compose the discipline studied. Model building as a science teaching strategy involves representing science content (concepts, phenomena, processes, and relationships) in concrete or abstract ways through developing, presenting, and discussing the content using visual images (drawings, pictures, videos, etc.), physical models and depictions, graphics, symbols, mathematical relationships, and verbal and nonverbal descriptions. Science teachers may provide models by using analogies. For example, teachers often depict equilibrium using a graphic or a verbal description of a balanced seesaw as an analogous phenomenon. Science concepts may be presented through "modeling" or representational modes to enable students to develop and retain understanding of the concepts. The models should help the students understand, explain, and apply the concepts related to the respective discipline. Earth science teachers may design lessons to help students develop mental models of plate tectonics or of the water cycle, while biology teachers can help students develop mental pictures of a DNA molecule or a simple ecosystem. Chemistry teachers may promote mental images of a sugar molecule, and physics teachers may promote the formation of mental pictures of the relationships among different waves of the visual spectrum. In any event, students have to develop the images themselves by their own mental processes. Teachers cannot transport the models or images intact from their mental perceptions to the students' mental structures. The longer blocks of instructional time provided in block schedules enable teachers to design the type of learning activities that help students develop the mental models and images that are important to science learning.

Harrison (1998, 421) relates that using models helps students learn to think critically and creatively as well as retain ideas. He also reports the some research studies show that students may mistakenly think of models as true pictures of nonobservable phenomena and concepts. Models should be viewed as scientists' and teachers' attempts to represent complex or abstract phenomena in a way that facilitates student understanding. Models are not "right answers."

The idea associated with developing mental models as an instructional strategy is that learning in science can be facilitated by engaging students in activities in ways that assist them to develop mental images of science related forms and structures, phenomena, processes, and the interrelationships among objects. Students may be able to form the images in their minds as a result of experiences that do not involve direct observations of the actual objects, substances, and events. For example, chemistry teachers may provide lessons to help students develop and hold mental images of particular atoms and molecules and their effects on one another. They do this not by having students actually observe the atoms and molecules but by engaging the students in other activities for creating the images. Examples such as those in Figure 3.9 are readily available in textbooks and other sources.

FIGURE 3.9 TWO ATOMS

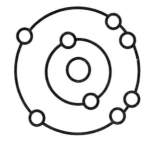

Hydrogen Atom

Oxygen Atom

Science teachers help students develop mental pictures and models by representing concepts in pictorial, graphic, three-dimensional, and mathematical ways when they discuss or present the concepts. The students may actually sketch, describe, or otherwise represent their own mental pictures of the concepts studied. Students may also enjoy and learn from kinesthetically representing (through dance or body movements) phenomena and relationships among objects in science. After students produce or simulate their mental images and representations, they and the teacher can discuss them and suggest adjustments to assist in developing more accurate or appropriate physical representations and mental images and understandings. Glynn (1997) states that drawing mental models helps students in the science disciplines to consolidate information about concepts and identify misconceptions.

> After learning about gaseous compounds, for example, one student drew a mental model of a methane (CH_4) molecule. Her model was almost correct but lacked one of the four hydrogen atoms. When she discussed the model with her teacher, she explained that she confused the molecular formula for methane with that of another molecule in the lesson, ammonia (NH_3). A student who was interested in plant and animal cells drew a mental model of an animal cell. While his drawing was generally representative of an animal cell, it incorrectly included a cell wall. When he discussed his model with his teacher, the student explained that he thought the animal cell had a wall because "the membrane [alone] couldn't keep all the stuff inside the cell. (Glynn, 1997, 31)

Glynn (1997) indicates that having students draw mental models can serve as a diagnostic strategy for determining the students' level of understanding of a subject. Teachers can examine the students' representations of their mental images to detect gaps in their knowledge and misconceptions they hold. The following guidelines are for science teachers who wish to use the "model-building" technique.

♦ Draw or represent your mental models of concepts for students and report your thoughts when you introduce the concepts.

♦ When possible show several mental models to represent the same concept so that students understand that a model is a flexible tool for representing concept features, rather then the only way to represent the concept or its features.

♦ Have students draw or develop updated models of concepts as they learn more about them.

♦ Be sure to emphasize to students that the representations they provide should be original (their own mental images) rather than reproductions from other sources.

♦ Encourage students to clarify their representations by labeling features, drawing arrows, and providing other relevant details and explanations. (Remember that students may develop misconceptions that should be corrected.)

♦ Allow students to finish their representations before interrupting or correcting them.

♦ When appropriate, plan and present lessons that are multimedia events that include diagrams, photos, videos, and other visuals and objects.

♦ Make sure the classroom climate is conducive to artistic and other creative endeavors, a place where students are not reluctant to illustrate their products to represent their mental images. Students should not be judged by other people's standards of artistic and creative talent (Glynn, 1997, 32).

Modeling is a sophisticated thinking process that should be an explicit feature of the science curriculum. Teachers should be aware of the value of using models for science instruction, and they should give ample thought to how they use models, whether analogous, symbolic, theoretical, or mathematical models (Harrison, 1998, 420). Examples of models are shown in Figure 3.10.

Block schedules tend to allow time for students and teachers to develop their models, explain them, ask questions about them, and make needed adjustments in them all during a single class session. This results in the more efficient and effective use of time and better understanding of the concepts covered.

SOCRATIC SEMINARS

Socratic seminars are classroom discussions centered around a particular topic or set of questions posed by the teacher. Most of the dialogue in the discussion is among the students with the teacher serving as facilitator, clarifier, manager, and judge. (Ball and Brewer, 1996, 44). The participants are usually

FIGURE 3.10 EXAMPLES OF MODELING

♦ Mathematical model:

$$Specific\ Gravity\ =\ \frac{Weight\ of\ Sample\ in\ Air}{Weight\ of\ Equal\ Volume\ of\ Water}\ =\ \frac{Weight\ of\ Sample\ in\ Air}{Loss\ of\ Weight\ in\ Water}$$

♦ Graphical model:

Represent the density of an animal population using a line graph or represent the change in the growth of plants using a histogram (bar graph). (The graphs may be done using a computer.)

♦ A descriptive analogous model:

To convey functioning of cell using city example:

For urban students, a cell can be viewed as being like a city. Each cell organelle represents an office or building of responsibility within the city. The mitochondrion is the power plant, the lysosomes are the policemen, the endoplastic reticulums are the roads and streets, etc.

♦ Physical three-dimensional models:

To convey the relative sizes and distances in the solar system:

If "the sun were a pumpkin about a foot in diameter, Mercury would be a tomato seed about 50 feet away, Venus would be a pea about 75 feet away, Earth would be a pea about 100 feet away, Mars would be a little raisin about 175 feet away, Jupiter would be an apple about 550 feet away, Saturn would be a peach about 1025 feet away, Uranus would be a plum about 2050 feet away, Neptune would be a plum about 3225 feet away, and Pluto would be smaller than a strawberry seed nearly a mile away." (vos Savant, 2000, 15.)

Use pop beads to help teach genetic concepts such as mitosis, meiosis, haploid, diploid, homologue, tetrad, and sister chromatids. Pop beads are available with magnetic centromere that allows them to stick to a surface for easy viewing.

Use styrofoam balls and toothpicks to model atomic and molecular structures.

Play dough or similar materials can be used to represent land forms, cellular structures, and objects of the solar system.

♦ Physical movement and role-playing models:

Students can pretend to be a red blood cell traveling in the bloodstream of the body.

Several students may move to simulate the movement of the earth and moon in relationship to each other and the sun.

arranged in a circle or other pattern to allow them to look at each other (make eye contact) during discussions. In some cases, the seating arrangements may include an inner circle and an outer circle, with the inner circle comprised of discussants and the outer circle comprised of observer and potential discussants. Socratic seminars offer teachers an alternative for promoting thinking and discussion among student for reaching certain ends. The seminars promote student dialogue, thought, and ownership of learning. The seminar interactions also promote a sense of a community of learners among some students—a very positive effect.

Ball and Brewer (1996, 30) depict the seminars as activities to "generate thinking about" the ideas, principles, and applications of science. Class sessions in the block are more conducive to this strategy than class sessions in traditional schedules because the sessions are longer, and other introductory activities and/or closure activities can occur on the same day. As an example, Ball and Brewer indicate that "biology students may explore Rachael Carson's environmental treatise *Silent Spring* or an essay on genetic engineering." They also state that the seminar strategy works beautifully for humanities courses, but for some disciplines, including science, Socratic seminars offer only an occasional strategy "for teachers to use in making the content relevant and expandable." Therefore, Socratic seminars are not identified as strategies thatscience teachers will or should use often in the block. See Figure 3.11 for some ideas for Socratic seminars in science.

FIGURE 3.11 SOME SOCRATIC SEMINARS TOPICS

Science topics that may be appropriate for Socratic seminars include:
- The merits of feeding growth hormones and antibiotics to livestock
- Human population growth and the carrying capacity of the earth
- Fossil fuel use
- Recycling benefits and problems
- Waste disposal methods
- Radioactive and nuclear wastes
- Space exploration and travel
- Genetic engineering (foods and/or medicine)
- Greenhouse effects and global worming
- Energy sources and use
- Continental drift
- Lessons, if any, from the dinosaurs
- Evolution, evidence for the theory
- Using herbicides and pesticides

Ball and Brewer provide several guidelines for conducting Socratic seminars. In preparation for the seminars, teachers should:

- Select the appropriate seminar readings that are related to the prescribed curriculum.

- Define the objectives and outcomes for the seminars.

- Design preseminar and postseminar tasks for students, to prepare them and to bring closure at the end.

- Write the questions for opening, continuing, and closing the seminars. (It is the most important task for the success of the process).

Students should prepare for the seminars by:

- Reading the text or information assigned prior to the seminars. (They should take notes and think critically or reflect on the readings.)

- Completing all preseminar tasks.

BRAINSTORMING

Brainstorming is used to generate as many ideas as possible about a situation or problem in a short period of time. Science teachers may find brainstorming to be a viable technique at the beginning of an investigation, experiment, or field trip. The ideas generated during the brainstorming activities may include possible hypotheses, procedures (steps to solving a problem), or things to look for or make critical observations about. After a number of ideas or hypotheses are generated, teachers may provide guidance for the students to determine which of the ideas or hypotheses are more plausible. They can then rank the ideas and hypotheses according to plausibility and test them. For the procedure to work effectively, students must feel comfortable sharing ideas and having them scrutinized by other students and the teacher. Therefore, it is critical to facilitate an open and nonthreatening classroom environment. Suggestions are:

- Develop clear and explicit guidelines for the brainstorming sessions.

- Tell students not to criticize classmates.

- Make sure that everyone has the opportunity to provide input at least once during the discussion.

- Manage the session by giving each speaker a time limit. For example, each student might get 1 minute for the first speaking opportunity and, if time permits, 30 seconds for the second opportunity.

- Set a time limit for each brainstorming session before the session starts and adhere to it. A recommended amount of time for most sessions is 20 to 30 minutes. Every comment made and every question asked by students does not require a response from the teacher.

- Outline a procedure for using student input to rank the ideas generated. This is important if some of the ideas are to be pursued as experimental hypotheses and/or procedures.

After students become accustomed to the approach, brainstorming becomes easier to manage as an instructional approach. Lyons (1992, 11) suggests following a sequence of steps similar to the following for managing brainstorming activities.

1. Ask students to generate lists of questions, topics, hypotheses, or solutions depending on the objectives of the brainstorming activity.

2. Assign the students to groups of 3 to 5 members.

3. Allow the groups to generate their lists by writing them on large sheets of paper.

4. Post the lists on the walls with tape.

5. Allow the list entries to be explained or clarified but not evaluated.

6. Delete duplicate items listed (this may require some negotiation concerning the meaning of items).

7. Allow students to individually vote on the item rankings.

8. The teacher should tabulate the votes and report the results.

Almost any investigation or experiment can be preceded by a brainstorming sessions designed to help students identify viable courses of action and generate hypotheses. Listed next are some questions and problem-solving situations that students may approach through brainstorming exercises.

1. Ideas for improving water quality in the local area

2. The best design for a downhill boxcar

3. Design for an experiment for determining the best fertilizer for tomato plants

4. What to pack for a month-long trip to Mars

5. How to identify the best common building materials for absorbing and holding heat energy

6. Developing a plan for measuring the amount of particulate matter in the local atmosphere

7. How many moles of oxygen are in four breaths of air?

8. A procedure for determining the amount of water in a specific quantity of soil

GAMES AND PUZZLES

Games and puzzles are activities designed to be enjoyable for the students. They stimulate interest or motivate students and may contribute to the development of social and problem-solving skills as well as promote learning of science concepts. On occasion, the use of games and puzzles in the science classroom can be justified as controlled instructional "time-outs" or rewards for good performance. It is important, however, that the activities contribute to the lesson objectives and the development of skills, concepts, and attitudes related to the science discipline. In particular, games can be used to enrich, reinforce, and review content that has been covered in other ways. They can also be used as assessment tools for gaining information about students' levels of understanding and abilities to apply concepts in different contexts.

Because the class sessions in the block are relatively long, science teachers may find it helpful to integrate brief game and puzzle activities into the activities for some sessions. In many cases, students will be motivated to learn the content in order to perform well in the games. Some students are motivated by the competition and attention that games and puzzles generate, even when they may not be highly motivated by other class activities. Most students welcome games for changing the pace and as tension relievers.

Games and puzzles for science can be teacher-made or acquired from commercial companies. Teachers often develop science-type games based on popular games that students may know about. For example, science-related games similar to *Jeopardy, Trivial Pursuit, Monopoly*, and *Tic-Tac-Toe* have been designed for particular lessons or topics. The formats can include pencil-and-paper games, card games, board games, role-playing, simulations, material manipulations, and memory games. Some teachers have developed very successful learning activities around competitions such as having students design a bridge that will hold more weight than those built by classmates or designing a system for dropping an egg from a certain height without breaking it. The students are given specific construction parameters and conditions in attempts to make the contests fair. The activities are designed to get students to learn new concepts, apply concepts, and solve problems. In some cases, the activities are performed by individual students, whereas in others, students are assigned to groups to perform the activities. Figure 3.12 describes a science game.

Ellington, Addinall, and Percival (1981) discuss the value of using games and simulations for science instruction in their book *Games and Simulation in Science Education*. They provide examples of card and board games (pp. 35–76), suggestions for designing your own exercises (pp. 105–114), and information for evaluating games, simulations, and case studies (pp. 115–126). Because some of the information presented is outdated, teachers will need to choose carefully from the activities and adapt them to specific needs. Ellington et al. describe a board game called *The Great Blood Race*. The purpose of the game is stated as: to help students "appreciate the composition and circulation of blood in the human body, the main organs it visits and the reasons why, and some of the things that can go wrong with the circulation system." They describe a card game designed "to reinforce and consolidate basic ideas regarding the different types of atoms and ions and the ways in which they combine to form ionic and covalent chemical compounds." The game consists of 100 cards, each representing a type of atom or ion, a multiplier (2 or 3), or a joker. Each round of the game takes from 5 to 10 minutes and any number of rounds can be played. "The players are dealt hands of 10 cards and, playing in rummy fashion, have to try to get rid of their cards by forming valid chemical compounds. The winner of each round is the first player to get rid of all his cards, the other players collecting

FIGURE 3.12 EXAMPLE OF A GAME

At least two teams of players compete to identify the most substances, objects, or organisms in a given amount of time.

Objective

To identify the names of substances, objects, or organisms and match their names with their descriptions.

Materials

1. A stack of cards or paper squares with the names and/or pictures of the items the students are to learn. The stack should include only those items that belong in the study of the relevant topic. For example, stacks of cards for games might be composed of the names or pictures of:

   a. Elements of the periodic chart

   b. Organisms (to identify the names or phyla to which they belong)

   c. Rocks and minerals found in nature

2. Watch, clock or timer.

Rules

Each team of three or more players will take turns in the game. One player from the first team picks a card from the stack with the cards face down. He or she will try to communicate the identification or the name and/or picture on the card drawn using gestures and actions only. No words or drawings can be used. Spelling of the words or names is not allowed. Each team is given only two minutes to identify the item on the card. Those not identified should be placed in a different "used" stack than those that have been identified. Any number of points can be assigned for a correct identification as long as the points given are consistent. The members of a group will alternate to act out the identifications. The teacher should make the decision before the game begins concerning the total time that will be allotted and/or the total points needed for a team to win the game.

Suggestions for Other Competitive Games

1. Given a specific type and amount of materials, individuals, teams, or groups of students can compete to construct a:

   a. Kite that stays aloft the longest

   b. Paper airplane that glides the farthest

   c. Parachute that descends from a specific height with an object of a specific weight the slowest

   d. Bridge spanning a measured distance that supports the greatest weight

2. Which group can melt a cube of ice fastest without taking the cube from the dish or using a source of heat other than body heat?

3. Which team can grow the tallest plant in a certain amount of time (following specific guidelines)?

penalty points according to the number and type of cards they have left. The overall winner is the player with the smaller number of penalty points after a number of rounds have been completed." Figure 3.13 (pp. 92–93) shows an example of a science game, a crossword puzzle.

Web sites are available for generating crossword puzzles by entering the terms for inclusion along with the clues. The address for the site used to generate the puzzle in Figure 3.13 is http://puzzlemaker.school.discovery.com/ (Discovery Communications, Inc., 1999).

SIMULATIONS

A simulation is a representation of a real thing, process, procedure, or event. A simulation is usually designed and used to teach concepts and skills or to change attitudes and behaviors while avoiding the dangers, costs, and complexities of using the real thing or participating in the real event. When simulations are used in science classrooms, students get to take action in well-defined situations and model real-life reactions. They are able to assess the consequences of their actions in a safe environment. They can make adjustments based on the consequences and learn or practice for encountering similar situations later. In particular, simulations can be used effectively in science to develop laboratory skills.

As Morie (1996, 153) indicates, simulations are often used in science as a complementary and supportive strategy for reinforcing concepts and skills taught in other ways. Block schedules allow science teachers to integrate simulation activities into the instructional flow of lessons and class sessions by using them to transition from lectures and discussions to investigations and experiments or to alternate the sequence depending on the topic. Getting through the sequence of activities related to a topic or concept during one class session increases the potential for student learning and understanding.

Simulations can be used to help students develop knowledge while employing a constructivist or inquiry approach to instruction. For example, earth science students can develop understanding of the procedures used in measuring the depths of the ocean bottom and mapping the contours of the ocean floors, using a shoebox, plaster of paris, and soda straws. (Pettus, 1998, 24–27) In the example, a shoebox with lid is used to represent the ocean. The lid serves as the surface of the ocean. The plaster of paris is used to form shapes to simulate the ocean floor. When small holes are punched in the lid and the lid is placed on the box, students use the straws to determine the depths and shapes of the forms in the box while not being able to see in the box. As a result of the exercise, student develop understanding about how scientists may use weighted lines and echo-sounding devices to determine water depths and the profiles of the ocean bottoms.

Computer-based simulations create the potential to provide students with a variety of learning and enriching experiences. Programs are available that provide simulations concerning space flight, weather forecasting, ecology, genetics, chemical reactions, sound, and many other topics. Computer simulations will enable science teachers to use instructional time more efficiently, provide sophisticated learning activities in a safe manner, and allow for repetitions by students who need them. Computer simulations also offer teachers relatively authentic ways of assessing students' abilities to analyze, synthesize, and use the concepts and skills of science.

The following steps are suggested for using simulations in science:

1. Define the student objectives for the activity.

2. Prepare the materials and equipment that will be needed.

3. Introduce the activity and materials to students by sharing the objectives and giving needed directions.

4. Define the students' roles and outline the rules and guidelines for participation in the simulation.

5. Conduct the simulation or guide students through the activities.

6. Develop and ask students questions to facilitate discussion and closure, and to help students draw conclusions and generalizations.

While simulations are not substitutes for hands-on activities in science, they do help students to develop science concepts and learn to solve problems using logical and scientific methods. Science teachers should think about how best to integrate simulated activities into the curriculum to enhance student understanding of the science concepts where the hands-on activities are not practical. See Figure 3.14 (p. 94) for an example of a simulation activity.

(Text continues on page 94.)

FIGURE 3.13 AN EXAMPLE OF A CROSSWORD PUZZLE

Electricity and Magnetism

Across

4. The charge of a proton.
5. Measures of electrical potential energy.
8. Region in which certain physical effects of a magnet exist and can be detected.
9. Measures of electrical charge.
11. Readily transmits heat or electricity.
12. Unit for measuring rate of flow of electricity.
15. A unit of energy.
16. Natural electric discharge in the atmosphere.
18. The charge of an electron.
19. An atom with a net positive or negative charge.
22. Unit of electrical resistance.
23. Does not readily conduct electricity.

Down

1. Connection to the earth to neutralize charge on an object.
2. Matter burned to produce heat or mechanical energy.
3. Natural magnetic stone.
6. A part of a magnet where the force is the strongest.
7. A closed path followed by an electric current.
10. The force that is in a magnet.
13. Cylindrical coil of wire that resembles a bar magnet when carrying a current.
14. Safety device that prevents exceeding desired amperage.
17. A machine that produces electricity.
20. A flow of electric charge.
21. A unit of power for measuring electricity.

Answer key to Puzzle

1. Grounding	2. Fuel	3. Lodestone
4. Positive	5. Volts	6. Pole
7. Circuit	8. Field	9. Coulombs
10. Magnetism	11. Conductor	12. Ampere
13. Solenoid	14. Fuse	15. Joule
16. Lightning	17. Generator	18. Negative
19. Ion	20. Current	21. Watt
22. Ohm	23. Insulator	

FIGURE 3.14 EXAMPLE OF A SIMULATION ACTIVITY IN EARTH OR SPACE SCIENCE

Objective:

The student will be able to describe the rotation of the moon and how it revolves around the earth so that the same side is visible from the earth at all times.

Some students have difficulty understanding how the moon can rotate on its axis once as it revolves around the earth once (approximately 27 days and 8 hours) so the same side always faces the earth (the only side of the moon visible from the earth).

Materials: None

Procedure:

In pairs, have the students simulate the relative movements of the earth and the moon. The student designated as the earth will turn (rotate) slowly once over one minute (60 seconds) to equal one day, while the second student (moon) moves around the first student (earth) facing the earth at all times. Then, have the students exchange places and play the opposite role. Question the student about how many times the moon rotated on its axis during one revolution around the earth.

CASES AND SCENARIOS

A case or scenario is a brief description of an event or situation that presents a problem or concern. The problem or concern should be one that has potential solutions involving the application of science knowledge, skills, or methods that have been studied. A case can be based on a real occurrence, or the situation can be made up by the teacher or someone else to fit the objective to be served. In particular, environmental, agricultural, health, and nutritional situations tend to have implications for science study (see Figure 3.15). Cases can be used to:

- Develop awareness of issues.
- Teach content or promote understanding of concepts.
- Get students to apply concepts to realistic problems.
- Develop skills in decision making, critical thinking, and problem solving.
- Help students clarify their opinions and beliefs about concepts and issues.
- Assess levels of student understanding.
- Assess students' opinions and attitudes.

FIGURE 3.15 EXAMPLE OF A CASE

The Chemical Dilemma Scenario

Milton is a student in chemistry class. The class has studied about some chemical reactions and interactions involving combining substances (chemicals) to form new substances. Milton knows that some changes can be observed while they occur and some may be subtle or unobservable over a short period of time. For example, Milton now understands some practical reasons for combining substances, such as why soap and water may make a better cleaning agent for some purposes than water alone. He also knows why an acid solution (i.e., HCl) is used to test rocks for the presence of calcium carbonate and why iodine can be used to test for starch in foods.

One day when Milton's mother was cleaning the house, Milton noticed that she was using a scouring cleanser (powder) to clean a counter top. While the cleanser residue was still on the counter she began spraying the counter top with a liquid cleaner from a second container. *What, if any, reaction would you expect from Milton, even though he has not studied about the specific substances his mother is using? Why? Discuss your reasons.*

Ellington, Addinall, and Percival (1981) provide some ideas and suggestions that may be helpful for teachers to develop their own cases or scenarios. For example, a physics teacher may be able to describe the amount and types of energy used for heating and cooling the average home in the local area. The size (cubic feet of space, etc.) of the home to be heated and cooled, building materials, windows, and other features of the home would be included in the description. Information on the sources and costs of energy may be given in the description. The number of inhabitants and their behaviors and routines should be included. Some mention of the weather and climatic conditions should also be included, even if students will be required to collect the details as part of the case study process. The idea is to describe the situation for study as clearly as possible, while keeping the descriptions as brief as possible. The key question for students to consider is how to reduce the amount of energy used (and the cost to the inhabitants) in the home without reducing their comfort and convenience.

Suggestions for using cases:

♦ Choose brief descriptions of situations that do not involve highly controversial content (e.g., evolution versus creationism may be too controversial).

♦ Write or revise the situation to make it appropriate for the students and for meeting the instructional objective.

♦ Provide specific and clear directions for students to respond to the cases, such as, "State specifically what you would say or do if you saw the woman [in Figure 3.15] getting ready to mix the solutions." Why would you say that?

♦ Have students read and write their reactions and responses as individuals before discussing the cases as groups.

♦ Allow students to discuss the situations as groups of three or four and to determine whether they can reach consensus on a response or solution. Let the students know it is acceptable if consensus cannot be reached.

♦ Have each group report its results.

♦ Discuss the results and attempt to make any adjustments in the decisions (solutions) that concern application of the science concepts and processes studied. Strictly opinion issues that are not specifically related to the concepts should not be afforded valuable class time.

Remember that the students need to have the pertinent knowledge base before cases can be used effectively. Cases can also be time-consuming, so they are recommended for use occasionally rather than as the primary instructional approach. Teachers should carefully select or develop the cases to depict relevant situations and conditions. Cases can be difficult to manage in terms of guiding students toward the desired outcomes, as well as staying within a specific time frame, so good planning and skill in managing or focusing the ensuing discussions are imperative.

Science teachers can develop their own cases by beginning with a situation that poses a problem or dilemma needing a solution and requires applying the concepts and skills that the students have been exposed to in class. For example, after studying units on astronomy and the solar system, students may be expected to use their knowledge to attempt to determine directions. A case description can be developed concerning a person getting separated from a camping group in the late evening and desiring to find his or her way back to camp or to seek help.

Sources for cases may be located on Internet sites containing problem-solving activities for science. Several Internet sources for cases exist for college-level science students and classes. Some of the case descriptions at the sites listed next can be easily adapted for high school students.

♦ Problem-Based Learning, University of Delaware (1999)—
  http://www.udel.edu/pbl/

♦ Case Studies in Science Collection, University at Buffalo (1997)—
  http://ublib.buffalo.edu/libraries/projects/cases/ubcase.htm

♦ Critical Thinking in Biology: Case Problems (1999)—
  http://www.saltspring.com/capewest/ct.htm

Topics such as the following may provide ideas to help teachers develop their own cases related to the objectives and lessons they have developed for students.

- The case of the dying birds
- A case of finding directions at night after separation from other campers
- Real or hypothetical case of stream pollution
- The discovery of a new organism—how to classify it

FIELD TRIPS

Field trips are planned excursions for students outside the classroom setting. Field trips should relate to the content of other instruction going on during the time they are experienced. Worthwhile field trips are usually planned well and have specific instructional objectives just as other effective instructional strategies. Planning isolated field trips with no instructional objectives in mind is discouraged.

Science field trips should be planned to help students solve problems or answer questions that have been presented. The students should be aware of the purpose for the field trips and should have active roles in the planning and learning activities. Too often teachers fail to help students prepare for field trips beforehand, and students participate without being aware of the objectives (desired outcomes) for the trips. When that happens, the students regard the activities as noninstructional breaks. Consequently, teachers may have problems getting students to display desired behaviors during or after the trips. Science field trips should be planned to encourage student involvement in the related activities and encourage maximum learning from the activities. Students should be asked to observe, investigate, and record data for forming conclusions and meeting the objectives of the learning activities.

Science field trips can include trips outside the school building but still on the school campus. Trips of this nature can be taken frequently because they do not involve the transportation and legal liability problems associated with off-campus trips. Areas around the school building are often rich in learning resources. Even inner-city schools usually have environments outside the classrooms, which provide alternative setting and resources for instruction in science.

Block schedules are particularly conducive to on-campus field trips because they allow time for organizing the students in groups, giving directions, making observations, collecting specimen, recording data, and performing many other activities, all during the same class session rather than over several class sessions. Consequently, the trips become more authentic, and students are able to make better connections and develop better inferences and conclusions.

Field trips to environments and settings beyond the school campus usually involve additional planning for travel, safety, supervision, and meeting instructional objectives (see Figure 3.16). Consequently, the number of off-campus field trips possible during a given period of time is limited. Places to which science teachers have traditionally taken their students include museums, farms, factories, processing plants, parks, planetariums, and geologic sites. For

FIGURE 3.16 COMMON FIELD TRIP SITES

Place/Location	*Instructional Topics/Goals*
• Water treatment facilities	• Compounds, mixtures, solutions, water quality, water pollution
• Swimming pools	• Buoyancy with depth, density, specific gravity, refraction of light
• Geologic sites, exposed rock formations	• Sedimentation, geologic session
• Streams, lakes, and ponds	• Water pH, chemical properties, water quality, aquatic communities, human impact studies
• Science museums	• Motion studies, light, sound
• Zoos, aquariums, plant and animal reserves	• Organism diversity, animal behavior, taxonomy or classification of organisms
• Grassy and open areas	• Human impact study, species diversity
• Wooded area, forests, and parks	• Food chains and webs, energy pyramids, species diversity, ecology, populations
• Areas under development or recently developed	• Erosion, soil profiles, human impact studies, science and ethics, population studies
• Airports	• Physics—motion, aerodynamics, environmental impact study
• Farms	• Ecology, erosion, soils, biotechnology, genetic engineering, ethics and science
• Hospitals and doctors' offices	• Microbiology, bacteria and viruses, medicines, biochemical concepts
• Bottling company	• Polymer chemistry
• Planetariums	• Astronomy
• Engineering firm	• Physics of structures and design
• Food-processing plants (poultry/pork/beef)	• Food and energy, anatomy studies, health, diseases
• Colleges and universities	• Rock and mineral collections, specimen collections, use of and demonstrations of specialized equipment, information and demonstrations from experts
• Large parking lots/paved over areas	• Temperature changes, diversity of organisms, erosion
• Recycling plants, sewage treatment and waste disposal areas	• Energy use, waste disposal, recycling
• Power plants	• Energy use and conversion, conservation of energy, sources of energy
• Amusement parks (with roller coasters and other moving devices)	• Momentum, gravity, friction, kinetic and potential energy

the off-campus sites, it is motivational and memorable for students when an expert is on site to interact with them and answer their questions. However, teachers should discuss with students the acceptable behaviors for interacting with the experts and other individuals at the site.

Making the decision to take the class on a field trip

- What are the specific instructional objectives?
- Is the trip practical or justified based on the time involved, costs, safety, etc., or can the objectives be accomplished by the use of audio-visuals or other means?
- Will the trip enable students to be directly involved in activities that may result in learning of general and lasting value?
- What are the school system's policies and guidelines regarding instructional field trips?

Planning a field trip for your students

- Contact appropriate school authorities for permission to take the trip and to proceed with your plans.
- Contact the authorities of the site to be visited and get permission if the site is off-campus or requires permission.
- Visit the site to check on potential instructional, safety, and health factors.
- Schedule the specific field trip activities and arrange for transporting the students if transportation is required.
- Notify parents and give them the field trip schedule and other details. Get their consent for taking the students on the trip.
- Arrange for adequate supervision of the students while on the trip.
- Prepare the students for the trip
  - Discuss the purpose of the trip and write out questions to be answered or things to be accomplished.
  - Discuss the required standards of behavior and the learning behaviors expected of the students.
  - Give information on appropriate attire to be worn.
  - Provide any other pertinent details or requirements.

Supervising the field trip

- Arrive at the designated meeting place ahead of the students.
- Make sure you know which students are supposed to go on the trip and make a list of who actually shows up to take the trip.
- Invite a member of the administrative and/or supervisory staff to go along.
- See that all students are properly assigned to groups and have adequate adult supervision at all times.

♦ See that all students are properly attired and have the required resources and supplies for the trip.

♦ Keep activities on schedule and return from the trip by the predesignated time.

Following-up the field trip

♦ Review the objectives or the questions the trip was designed to address with the students.

♦ Have the students share their findings with each other and relate the outcomes to other lessons or learning experiences.

♦ Assess specific student outcomes of the activities and note any desired changes for future trips of the same type.

♦ Write thank-you notes to the field trip hosts, volunteers, supervisors, site experts and guides, and other appropriate persons.

♦ Occasionally, there are follow-up learning activities to be carried out by further communication with the hosts or site experts.

LEARNING CENTERS

Learning centers are used more widely in elementary than in secondary school science. The difference in use according to school levels may be due to the fact that secondary students typically switch classrooms and teachers for each discipline and class session. These changes limit the flexibility needed to allow students to work and do investigations in centers. A perceived difference in what are appropriate learning experiences for secondary and elementary school students may also account for the disparity. Teaching science courses in the block will afford science teachers more flexibility in designing and implementing activities that will enable them to design and use science learning centers.

A science learning center is an area in the classroom or building that is set up to allow students, as individuals or small groups, to engage in investigative exercises and activities at their convenience and at a pace comfortable to them. The center is organized to include the directions, questions, materials, and equipment needed by the students to complete the planned activities. The center is usually designed as an expansion or extension activity related to the science concepts taught at the time. Therefore, other students may continue to participate in different learning activities while the center participants are engaged in center activities.

Centers can offer the individual student opportunities to manipulate materials and equipment, make predictions, test hypotheses, solve problems, and draw conclusions in a nonthreatening, self-paced situation. Where equipment is in short supply, learning center activities can enable all students to experience science on a personal or individual basis.

Learning centers can serve different purposes. They may be used to

♦ Introduce or begin a lesson or unit

♦ Provide extension activities for lessons and units

♦ Allow exploration and creative activities

♦ Assess student understanding and ability to apply skills and concepts

Introductory centers that are used to introduce lessons and units are designed to pique interest in the topic or lesson. The activities should be enjoyable for the students and may be designed to raise questions that the students will seek answers to in subsequent class activities. *Extension centers* are designed to provide extension and reinforcement activities to a lesson or other class activities. The activities in the extension center should be planned to relate directly to and expand on the prior learning. Often they are designed for the students who complete the regular lesson activities early; all students are not expected to participate. *Exploration centers* may be set aside for students to learn new information and develop creative ideas through reading and interacting with materials located in the center. In these centers, students may develop ideas and plans for doing science projects. Their explorations and work may result in creative designs, proposals, and actions for developing science fair projects. *Assessment centers* are planned and set up with activities and exercises for the students to work through. The activities and exercises require the use and application of skills and concepts covered in prior lessons. The teacher may attempt to assess the students' skill and performance levels as they work through the center tasks. The teacher may also assess the results of the students' center performances (the answers and products the student produce).

Suggested guidelines for planning and using science centers:

♦ Provide explicit objectives for the student before permitting the student to work at the center.

♦ Provide clear steps and directions for the student.

♦ Monitor the center to make sure conditions are safe.

♦ Set up the center in an area free of traffic and congestion.

♦ Allow for student movement to and from the center to participate in other class activities.

♦ Establish rules of behavior and conduct for participating in center activities.

♦ Make sure the center has appropriate workspace for the students.

♦ Make sure all needed materials and equipment are available.

♦ Replenish consumable materials as needed.

♦ Develop a plan for allowing all students opportunities to work through center activities.

♦ Develop and implement a plan for determining student performance during the activities, if desired.

Figure 3.17 describes some topics suitable for science learning centers.

FIGURE 3.17 SUGGESTED TOPICS FOR LEARNING CENTERS

◆ For earth science

Identification of rocks and minerals

- Provide directions for observing and recording the characteristics of various rock and mineral samples located in the center. Students will be expected to make the correct observations and recordings and utilize available reference sources to identify the rocks and minerals.

◆ For Biology

Food webs and chains

- Provide several large groups of organisms that can be found in different ecosystems (i.e., marine, forest, aquatic, desert, and grassland ecosystems) and have students as individuals or in small groups form food/energy webs including the organisms in each group. The names and/or pictures of the organisms can be used and the students may be asked to form the webs on paper or form the webs by connecting the center words or pictures by string provided in the center.

◆ For Chemistry

Acids and bases

- Provide solutions that include acids and bases, along with pH indicator paper or a pH meter, and have students identify the group to which they belong. Give directions for students to use various concentrations of the solutions to observe the changes.

◆ For Physics

Effects of the string length on the period of a pendulum

- Provide materials and directions for students to make a pendulum and a timing device. Direct students to alter the length of the pendulum system and make a graph depicting the relationship of the length to the period (time it takes to swing in one direction and back) of the pendulum. Ask students to describe the relationship.

PROJECTS

Projects are individual or group activities involving experimentation and investigation by the students to answer a question or solve a problem. The students perform the activities under the supervision and guidance of the science teacher. If they are student projects, the activities should be planned, carried out, and evaluated by the students. The most valued projects are those derived from student interest and students' desire to pursue or extend their knowledge and understanding beyond what has been gained in a teacher-directed lesson or unit. Therefore, projects are not considered a frontline strategy for science instruction. However, some science teachers assign projects to students whether they are interested in doing a project or not. Such assignments often do not develop into valuable learning experiences. Students should do projects because they desire to do them and want to learn something. Otherwise, the activities become assignments rather than projects. This is not to imply that science teachers should not encourage students to do projects and work independently. The teachers should provide encouragement, support, and guidance. However, the students need to be ready to accept most of the responsibility for completing the projects they choose to do. Projects and independent study activities tend to work best for honors and advanced placement classes, especially after the students have completed the required tests and examinations related to their placement performance and status. In any case, teachers should make sure students are being realistic by posing a few questions before encouraging them to do projects. Teachers may wish to ask:

- What is the purpose or objective of the project?
- Why do you think it is worthwhile to pursue the project?
- Is the project reasonable in terms of time, effort, cost, and available resources?

Doing projects enables students to learn to use the scientific method by experience. Teachers may encourage student projects by:

- Employing inquiry approaches in teaching
- Suggesting readings and ideas to students that may be of interest to them and cause them to be curious
- Suggesting ideas for projects but make it clear that students can reject the ideas as activities in which they wish to participate
- Being supportive and encouraging when students try activities not assigned
- Outlining the procedures students should follow in doing projects
- Providing help, support, and guidance when students decide to proceed with a project
- Allowing students to share their progress, successes, and findings with other students
- Evaluating students' projects based on quality of work, procedures, and knowledge gained rather than simply on project outcome (experimental conclusion)

Cothron, Giese, and Rezba (1993, 58) suggest the following format for students to use in writing a report on their science projects.

1. Title
2. Introduction

3. Experimental Design

4. Procedure

5. Results

6. Conclusion

INDEPENDENT STUDY

Independent study allows a student to experience working independently or as a separate individual to accomplish a goal. The student may design activities or search for information and evidence without ongoing assistance from the teacher or anyone else. Independent study is a way to help students to become self-confident, self-directed, and responsible. However, students need to be mature enough already to be successful at independent study if it involves a complex project or assignment. Long and involved projects can be very difficult and frustrating for many students, especially the less mature ones. Younger students and students who have not worked independently before may require more teacher guidance and assistance for success. Students should begin with and complete short, well-defined, independent study projects before attempting more long-term studies. For independent study, students should also try to identify real-life problems and issues that are relevant to them. If the topics and issues are relevant to them, the students will be motivated to complete the studies and do them well.

HOMEWORK

Homework assignments should be designed as integral parts of the instructional strategies and learning experiences for students in science. Therefore, science teachers should make meaningful assignments that will contribute to student learning. Homework should not be assigned as punishment or as exercises to keep students busy. The exercises should be directly related to the other ongoing instructional activities and may serve to introduce students to new information or to reinforce the learning of important science concepts and skills.

In block schedules, science teachers need to be sensitive to the resources and time constraints for students. An alternate-day schedule does not afford students additional time for science homework any more than it provides extra instructional time. However, the time allotted for the activities is organized in different ways. If the students are in class for 120 minutes for one session during a two-day period instead of 60 minutes for each of two sessions during a two-day period, the total time allotted is the same. Likewise, if students study and complete homework for a science course, they may be able to allot time to the course one evening out of the two available for a longer period of time. The other option for students is to divide the time among the two evenings and follow the same pattern for their remaining courses. On a four-by-four schedule, students may be able to allot more time to each course per evening because they are enrolled in fewer courses during the semester. However, no more time is available for doing homework assignments during the semester. Science teachers should be aware of these conditions and design homework assignments accordingly.

Teachers should make sure that homework assignments are clearly understood by the students. Clear and concise directions for doing the assignments should be provided, along with the purpose of the assignments and information on their relationship and relevance to other learning activities. If the assignments are considered important, teachers should take time to discuss them and to answer students' questions concerning the specific requirements for completing the tasks. Science teachers should not make the assignments at the very end of the instructional period or sessions, when it is usually difficult to focus student attention on such tasks.

Some homework assignments can be designed to allow students to take advantage of the unique resources they have available at home or in their community. Some activities can be designed to involve family members or members of the community. Such activities can be motivational for students and promote improved relationships with and support from parents and others. However, teachers should be sensitive to the different home environments and resources available to students. If differentiated assignments are made for different students, it should be clear to the students why the tasks are different for different individuals and how the assignments will contribute to their learning and development in science.

Teachers should indicate how the completed homework will be scored and how the scores will contribute to the overall performance grades for students. All homework assignments should be reviewed or assessed by the teachers, and feedback should be given to students in the form of comments and/or grades. The feedback should be timely and designed to help students learn the content of the course. Science teachers should be cautious about using homework assignments as the primary assessment strategies or tasks for judging course performance. The differences in resources and support that are available to different students in their homes cause equity and fairness concerns.

Science teachers should also be cautious about making out-of-class assignments for groups of students, requiring students to get together during times other than class time. Some students will experience difficulty meeting with their groups, and adequate supervision of student groups for such activities may present problems.

While it is advisable to give students exciting and motivational homework assignments, science teachers must exercise care not to give assignments that are potentially dangerous to students, family members, or others. Assignments involving working with chemical substances, sharp tools, electrical devices, animals, and making specimen collections outdoors are among the activities that pose potential risks for students.

To make meaningful and appropriate homework assignments, science teachers should:

- Determine the purpose of the assignments. Are they to be introductory and motivational, key learning activities, reinforcement or practice activities, supplements to other class activities, or assessment activities?

- Provide clear directions, descriptions, and examples. Students need to know specifically what they are expected to accomplish and the conditions under which they are to accomplish the tasks. Is receiving help allowed? How much time should be allotted? Can other resources and references be used?

- Identify homework assignments that are interesting and relevant to the students' lives, if possible. All valuable homework does not have to be boring and tedious for students.

- Make the assignments as meaningful to the students as possible, especially if they are long-term assignments—those that may involve activities lasting over a period of five days or more.

- Grade or mark the completed assignments and provide credit for the products based on quality, difficulty, and time required. Let students know ahead of time specifically how the products will be scored and judged and how the results will affect performance grades.

- Avoid making homework assignments that require special equipment or resources that all students do not have available in their environments.

- Avoid making homework assignments that are potentially dangerous.

- Do not use homework assignments as punishment activities. Students should view homework assignments as valuable activities that contribute to learning the course content.

Figure 3.18 is an example of a homework assignment.

FIGURE 3.18 EXAMPLE OF A RELEVANT AND APPLICATION HOMEWORK ASSIGNMENT

Chemicals at Home

Now that you have almost completed the chemistry course, you should have some knowledge and skills that you did not possess before the course. It is expected that you will be able to use some of what you have learned in your daily life. As an example of the use you might make of your learning, you may have become more discerning about the way chemical substances are stored and used in your home.

Your Assignment

1. List at least 10 chemicals and chemical substances that you can locate in your home. The list should include at least two products from each of the following categories: food and food preparations, medicine and health-care products, grooming and personal-care products, and cleaning and home-care products.

2. After the name of each substance, list the active or potentially active chemicals the substance contains.

3. Develop two lists: one containing the chemicals and chemical substances that you know something about relative to their chemical and/or physical properties, and the other containing the chemicals and chemical substances that you know nothing about.

4. Beside each substance that you know something about, state those properties you think the substance possesses. For the substances you know nothing about, indicate what you think their properties are based on their use or where they were found (located).

5. What suggestions do you have concerning the storage and/or use of the chemicals found in your home? Give reasons for your suggestions based on the chemical and physical properties of the substances.

Caution: Do not mix, taste, or otherwise test any of the substances for this assignment.	**Conditions:** You have two weeks (until May 15) to complete the assignment. The finished product should be typed or neatly written.

4

EVALUATION AND ASSESSMENT IN SCIENCE AND THE BLOCK SCHEDULE

Student assessment and evaluation serve the purposes of determining what the student knows and can do, determining the student's status and progress toward meeting instructional goals, determining how the student approaches a problem or task, motivating the student, and evaluating instructional methods and activities. Depending on the situation, the results of student assessments may be shared with the student, parents, other educators, other educational agencies, and potential employers. The assessment results may be used for future instructional planning, assigning students to groups and tasks, determining instructional and program accountability, and making other decisions.

ASSESSMENT AND THE INSTRUCTIONAL PROCESS

Effective assessment of student performance is critical when teaching in block schedules. Because instructional periods are concentrated, it is important for the teacher to know what the student can do and understand at any given time in order to take full advantage of the instructional time. Without effective assessment strategies, the teacher risks covering content the student has already mastered, covering content the student does not have the prerequisite knowledge and skills to master, or pacing the learning activities too fast or too slow. In either instance, the instructional time may not be used efficiently and effectively.

This chapter is designed to help the science teacher functioning in the block to review evaluation and assessment concepts in the context of utilizing extended blocks of time but not necessarily more instructional time overall. In

109

that context, assessment and assessment activities are more likely to be planned for a portion of a class session rather than the entire session.

The teacher should be mindful of the role assessment should play in the instructional process (Figure 4.1).

FIGURE 4.1 BASIC COMPONENTS OF THE INSTRUCTIONAL PROCESS

Goals & Objectives → Pre-assessment → Learning Activities → Assessment & Evaluation

A teacher is responsible for assessing student performance in a number of ways during instruction. This is done to accommodate students who have different learning styles, abilities, and backgrounds. By gathering assessment information in a variety of ways and concerning different aspects of the student's learning and development, the teacher is able to adapt the instruction to be most effective. A teacher may do preassessments to ascertain the student's level of performance and understanding prior to instruction. This may be done in an informal and nonstructured manner, or it may be a formal and structured activity.

Science teachers may perform assessments prior to providing instruction for a topic or unit of content to gather information about the students' prerequisite or preexisting knowledge, skills, and attitudes. The preassessments may also be used to help identify problems or special needs that individual students have that will have implications for instruction. The assessments that precede instruction in this manner may be referred to as *diagnostic assessments*.

As stated in Chapter 2, the assessments that the teacher does during instruction to make adjustments in the instruction are called *formative assessments*. These assessments also can be *formal* or *informal*. The teacher may develop or identify structured procedures for collecting and analyzing information and feedback from the student while a lesson or unit of materials is covered. The formal procedures may include anecdotal comments, observational checklists, workshops, and the like. The teacher may also informally devote attention to the student's questions, comments, behaviors, and responses and draw inferences for making adjustments in the instruction. These unstructured and incidental assessments are called informal assessments. A teacher tends to make informal assessments whether planned or not; therefore, it is important for the teacher to give attention to being objective and fair in making informal assessments.

Assessments done at the end of a unit of instruction that are used to summarize a student's performance regarding the content or to infer a student's level of mastery of the content are referred to as *summative assessments*. Summative assessments tend to receive the most attention, especially from students and parents, because the grades assigned to students for marking periods and courses are usually more heavily affected by summative assessments. Summative assessments may be done in a variety of forms including pencil-and-paper tests, written papers or reports, oral reports or interviews, performance tasks, portfolios, and projects. Many authorities in science education are advocating a shift toward assessment tasks that require students to use the knowledge and skills gained to solve problems, design experiments, develop models, interpret information, and draw conclusions, and a shift away from reliance on the traditional multiple-choice and true/false tests.

ASSESSMENT METHODS AND STRATEGIES

In the interest of aligning student assessment methods and measures with the learning activities, teachers should adapt assessments to determine if students can perform important operations and tasks rather than continue to administer traditional tests and assessments that focus only on facts and low-level cognitive skills. Block schedules afford the teacher the flexibility to use a variety of assessment methods for a unit of content. Using a variety of assessment methods increases the potential of accurately assessing the performance levels of all students regardless of learning styles, cultural backgrounds, and so forth. Variety in assessment techniques also helps to ensure consistency of assessments with instructional activities and objectives, including those that require high-level cognitive and psychomotor operations from students.

Broadly interpreted, assessment strategies and formats vary widely based on their purpose and the student traits, knowledge, or abilities to be assessed. Tests and testing as used in this chapter are not limited to pencil-and-paper cognitive tests that are objectively scored, but may include rating scales, checklists, survey inventories, and measures and formats for assessing affective and psychomotor performances as well. Assessment instruments and strategies for determining student achievement in science may include tests, as well as other performance-assessment alternatives. Many of the categories of the assessment options are given in Figure 4.2.

MATCHING ASSESSMENTS TO INSTRUCTION AND OBJECTIVES

To enable valid assessments, the assessment strategies must be based on what is required by the instructional objectives. The science teacher is responsible for ensuring that all aspects of the instructional process have a degree of consistency while also ensuring that the process is dynamic. The instructional objectives should directly influence the instructional content and methodologies and also the nature and content of assessments. Objectives are identified and stated to provide direction for instruction and to make evaluation meaningful. If the instructional objectives are changed, it is expected that planned

Figure 4.2 Classroom Assessment Methods

- ◆ Student tests
  Selected response formats
  - Multiple-choice
  - True/false
  - Matching

  Constructed response formats
  - Completion
  - Short answer
  - Essay answer
- ◆ Student tasks
  Student products
  - Models
  - Research papers
  - Portfolios
  - Science projects
  - Journals

  Student performances
  - Oral presentations
  - Laboratory demonstrations
  - Operating equipment
  - Role playing
- ◆ Observations
  Systematic observations
  - Oral questions and interviews
  - Checklists
  - Running records

  Incidental observations
  - Anecdotes
  - Leadership activities
  - Class participation
  - Collaboration with others
- ◆ Self-Reports
  Solicited responses
  - Attitude surveys
  - Questionnaires
  - Interest inventories
  - Sociometric devices

instructional strategies and content will be altered, and that the planned assessments will also change to determine when and if the objectives have been attained. Too often teachers develop and write down specific instructional objectives only to put them aside and teach and assess students in ways not entirely consistent with the objectives. Developing and using a grid or matrix, such as the one in Figure 4.3, will help science teachers to keep the instructional activities and assessment activities congruous.

FIGURE 4.3 INSTRUCTIONAL ALIGNMENT MATRIX

Objectives	Teaching/Learning Activities	Assessment/Evaluation Items, Tasks, & Procedures
1. The student will be able to illustrate the direction of matter and energy flow in an ecosystem.	Discuss how food and energy flows in an ecosystem. Provide familiar examples. a. Photosynthetic organisms to herbivores to carnivores and decomposers. b. Activity on relative numbers of organisms in populations on size and how they obtain their food.	Present the student with the names of organisms known to exist in a given ecosystem (e.g., deciduous forest). Ask the student to illustrate (e.g., using a web diagram) the usual direction(s) of matter and energy flow among the organisms.
2. The student will be able to interpret a line graph showing changes in a population over time.	Show how changes in several animal populations can be represented using line graphs. Instruct student groups to estimate population sizes of yeast cultures, record the data, and develop line graphs to represent the changes.	Present the student with a graph depicting changes in the human population over the last two centuries. Ask the student to describe in writing the changes in the human population over the time.
3. Others		

If the objective calls for the student to be able to *illustrate* the flow of energy, it seems impossible to assess his ability to illustrate the phenomenon by having him respond to a multiple-choice item such as:

Which of the organisms listed below is a tertiary consumer?
a. Mushroom
b. Hawk
c. Squirrel
d. Oak tree

In the block schedule, science teachers should focus on identifying what things are important for the students to learn and be able to do, with emphasis on the long-term value for the students. The question that should be asked often is, "What are the important skills, concepts, and generalizations for students to learn about this topic or unit?" Then the teacher should identify the best or most effective ways of determining when the students have attained the important things. (Of course, instruction will take place prior to implementing the assessment plan.) The important things identified should include the total of the area of student learning, not just cognitive memory components. They should include the processes of science, scientific attitudes and laboratory skills, as well as knowledge of science facts.

PERFORMANCE-BASED ASSESSMENTS

Performance-based assessments are important for implementing the type of science instruction being advocated as appropriate for students, especially where block scheduling has been implemented. Science and the learning of science are described as dynamic processes requiring active participation by those persons involved. They are much more than rote learning that can be assessed by paper-and-pencil tests. Therefore, the assessments utilized, as well as the objectives, should include important skills, understandings, and attitudes related to the science discipline studied.

Rudner and Boston (1994, 7) imply that performance assessments are constructivist learning experiences, as well as assessment devices. They require students to apply thinking skills, understand the nature of quality performance, and provide feedback to themselves and others. The experiences tend to empower students and teachers alike.

The terms *alternative assessment, authentic assessment,* and *performance assessment* are sometimes used as if they were synonymous. Alternative assessment refers to any assessments that differ from the multiple-choice, one-shot, paper-and-pencil measures that have been widely used in education. Authentic assessment refers to assessments that invite students to apply their knowledge and skills in ways they would in "real world" situations beyond school. Performance assessment is interpreted as a broader concept that may include features of alternative assessment and authentic assessment. Performance assessments require students to create answers or products that demonstrate their knowledge and skills. In a chemistry class,

Students might be asked to identify the chemical composition of a premixed solution by applying tests for various properties, or they might take samples from local lakes and rivers and identify pollutants. Both assessments would be performance-based, but the one involving the real-world problem would be considered more authentic. (Rudner and Boston, 1994, 2)

Performance-based tasks vary in authenticity. An assignment to "write a paper on pollution" is relatively inauthentic. An assignment to "write a proposal to correct a hypothetical pollution problem for a fictitious town" is somewhat authentic. While an assignment "to identify a pollution problem near your home, investigate the problem, determine what is needed to correct the problem, and write to local officials about correcting the problem" may be quite authentic.

Performance assessments may focus on students' products such as papers, reports, and projects; students' skills such as communication and psychomotor performances; or a combination of the two. To be effective, performance assessments in science usually have at least three components. They are:

1. A *task* that poses a meaningful problem and that has a solution requiring the student to use concrete materials

2. A *format* for the student's response

3. A *scoring system* that involves judging not only the right answer, but also the reasonableness of the procedure used to carry out the task (Ruiz-Primo and Shavelson, 1996, 1046)

The basic steps listed next will assist a teacher in designing an integrated performance assessment system:

- Identify desired goals and objectives
- Establish standards
- Identify the needed resources
- Design and implement the appropriate instruction
- Design the assessment tasks
- Design the scoring methods
- Decide on the follow-up steps to the assessment based on different outcomes

The problems and limitations associated with performance assessments relate to concerns about their reliability, fairness, and validity, along with the amount of time required to administer and score the students performances and performance results.

Performance assessments related to the following tasks may be used:

- Operating instruments of science
- Setting up apparatus
- Classifying and organizing materials

- Making accurate observations
- Forming logical inferences
- Planning and conducting experiments
- Forming and testing hypotheses
- Gathering and recording data
- Organizing and analyzing data
- Drawing conclusion based on data collected
- Developing and interpreting charts and graphs
- Doing library and on-line research
- Constructing models
- Writing reports of investigations and experiments

Performance-based assessments require that students have the opportunity to perform tasks that are evaluated based on some criteria used to determine proficiency. In addition to the activities already mentioned, tasks requiring concept mappings, journals, oral interviews, problem sets, and portfolios may be used in science for performance-based assessments The scoring system may include rubrics or rating scales that call for holistic or analytic scoring (see Figures 4.4 and 4.5).

JOURNALS AND PORTFOLIOS

Journals are diaries or logs kept by students chronicling observations, activities, and thoughts or reflections experienced in the science course. They provide sequential records to which the students can refer at any time. Making assignments for students to keep journals may be done for a unit, a grading period, or for the entire semester. Teachers need to check the journals at brief periods, depending on the schedule (at least weekly), to make sure students are making entries as prescribed.

Teachers may use student journals to assess how well the students are keeping up with class activities and providing comments to indicate their interpretations of the activities. If science teachers plan to use student journal entries as significant summative assessment tools, they should provide specific directions and guidelines for students concerning what things to include and how they should be entered. The students should be informed about expectations and how the journals will be graded at the beginning. Providing students with the specific criteria that will be used for the assessments will be helpful.

Portfolios are collections of students' work, usually related to a particular subject or skill area. They provide a broad picture of individual student performance because the work is done over a period of time. Portfolios may allow students to evaluate their own work as they select, revise, and place their work in their portfolios. Pheeney (1998, 36) defines student portfolios as collections of

(Text continues on page 119.)

FIGURE 4.4 EXAMPLE OF HOLISTIC RUBRIC
(SCORING SCALE) FOR PERFORMING AN EXPERIMENT

The teacher decides whether the student's performance is "excellent," "proficient" or "inadequate" based on his observations without rating each contributing criterion or indicator. Actually, the teacher may score the performance without the use of criteria or indicators, though it is not recommended.

Performance on Experiment

♦ ___ Excellent
- Clearly identified and recorded the problem/question.
- Developed reasonable hypothesis consistent with problem/question.
- Plan/design allowed appropriate comparison of variables.
- Controls and/or standards were used appropriately.
- Tests and manipulations performed carefully and accurately.
- Data and observations recorded accurately and in acceptable form.
- Formed conclusions based the data and provided supporting evidence.

♦ ___ Proficient
- Identified and recorded an acceptable problem/question.
- Developed a workable hypothesis.
- Plan/design reasonable to produce usable results.
- Recognized the need for controls and/or standards.
- Tests and manipulation were completed.
- Data and observations based on the tests were recorded.
- Formed conclusions but not entirely consistent with problem/hypothesis/findings.

♦ ___ Inadequate
- Failed to state or record explicit problem or question.
- No hypothesis development was evident.
- Failed to develop a plan/design for doing the experiment.
- The need for control or use of standard was not evident.
- Tests and manipulations were conducted haphazardly.
- Data and observations were not recorded or not meaningful.
- Failed to reach conclusions or conclusions were not supported by data.

FIGURE 4.5 EXAMPLE OF ANALYTICAL RUBRIC (SCORING SCALE) FOR PERFORMING AN EXPERIMENT

In analytical scoring, the individual components of the tasks are broken down and given descriptive indicators that are assigned values to allow rating the student's performance on each component. Then the ratings are summed to get the total score. This type of scoring is considered more accurate and fair, though it may be more time-consuming.

Performance on Experiment

(3) Clearly identified and recorded the problem/question.

(2) Identified and recorded an acceptable problem/question.

(1) Attempted to identify problem/question but needs work.

Points ____   (0) Failed to state or record explicit problem or question.

(3) Developed reasonable hypothesis consistent with problem/question.

(2) Developed a workable hypothesis.

(1) Hypothesis written but not appropriately.

Points ____   (0) No hypothesis development was evident.

(3) Plan/design allowed appropriate comparison of variables.

(2) Plan/design reasonable to produce usable results.

(1) Plan/design developed but inadequately.

Points ____   (0) Failed to develop a plan/design for doing the experiment.

(3) Controls and/or standards were used appropriately.

(2) Controls and/or standards applied but need adjustments.

(1) Recognized the need for controls and/or standards but not implemented.

Points ____   (0) The need for control or use of standard was not evident.

(3) Tests and manipulations performed carefully and accurately.

(2) Tests and manipulation were completed.

(1) Tests and manipulations were completed but more precision needed.

Points ____   (0) Tests and manipulations were conducted haphazardly.

(3) Data and observations recorded accurately and in acceptable form.

(2) Data and observations based on the tests were recorded.

(1) Some data and observations recorded but inaccurate and/or incomplete.

Points _____ (0) Data and observations were not recorded or not meaningful.

(3) Formed conclusions based data and provided supporting evidence and explanations.

(2) Formed conclusions consistent with data and problem.

(1) Formed conclusions but not entirely consistent with data and problem.

Points _____ (0) Failed to reach conclusions or conclusions were not supported by data.

Point   Comments:

Total _____

___

the students' work along with comments and reactions of others, including the teachers, parents, and peers. They can be in the form of file folders, three-ring binders, scrapbooks, or boxes. Portfolios may be different from journals in that journals are written records or logs of experiences and observations made by students concerning classroom activities or class assignments. Much depends on the purpose of the portfolios.

Portfolios may serve slightly different purposes in different situations. Three types of portfolios based on the purposes they are to serve are described next.

- *Showcase portfolios* contain the student's best works, which are usually selected by the student. Showcase portfolios contain finished products (papers, projects, etc.). Because the works are selected and organized by the student, showcase portfolios may be difficult and time-consuming for the teacher to assess. The emphasis is usually on the individual student's performance and best work rather than growth and progress. They can be used for evaluative or other purposes.

- *Documentation portfolios* (or working portfolios) contain examples of a student's work selected by the student and the teacher. They may contain a variety of products from class activities and assignments, including those that are in progress and finished reports of experiments and investigations, worksheets, rating forms, tests, and so forth. The emphasis is usually on the performance and progress of the student in relation to the instruction provided. Documentation portfolios may not be used for summative evaluation.

♦ *Evaluation portfolios* are usually more standardized across students in the class than other types because the teacher is interested in assessing student learning relative to some specific instructional objectives. Therefore, the emphasis is on the individual student's performance and progress toward attainment of the identified learning objectives. Evaluation portfolios provide records of performance and progress and may include results of tests and other assignments. They are used as evaluative tools.

The use of portfolios to assess student performance and progress may cause concern for some people because of scoring difficulties, reliability and validity issues, the amount of time required for the assessment process, and difficulties associated with communicating the information to parents and others. The scoring of portfolios tends to be more subjective than the scoring of test results and other assessments. There is a lack of consensus concerning how to attend to reliability and validity issues as they relate to portfolio and certain other performance-assessment strategies.

The following are some guidelines for planning and using student portfolios:

♦ Make sure the objectives and/or outcomes for the portfolios are clear.

♦ Make sure the uses to be made of the portfolios are understood.

♦ Provide guidelines for selecting and including information and materials.

♦ Let students know if they are to provide reflective statements and self-assessments concerning portfolio entries.

♦ Plan and arrange for periodic conferences with student concerning their portfolios.

♦ Develop scoring procedures and evaluative criteria that are clear, giving attention to fairness, reliability and validity issues.

Pheeney (1998, 37) suggests considering the following questions before using portfolio assessment:

♦ What is the primary purpose of the portfolio?

♦ What type of portfolio do I need?

♦ Which inclusions will meet the purpose of the portfolio?

♦ Which inclusions are compulsory?

♦ Will a scoring rubric be required?

It is suggested that a student self-assessment form or format be provided for students to evaluate the completeness of their work, assess their understanding of the unit of work concepts, reflect on the value of the experience, and raise questions they may have. The students may use copies of the same form used by the teacher (see Figure 4.6).

FIGURE 4.6 EXAMPLE: EVALUATION PORTFOLIO ASSIGNMENT AND RUBRIC FOR UNIT ON WEATHER

Objectives:
1. Demonstrate knowledge of the major factors affecting weather by using data on atmospheric, geologic, and other variables to discuss weather conditions.
2. Identify instruments used to measure variables related to atmospheric and weather conditions.
3. Identify and describe effects of weather on the activities and behaviors of people.

Assignment:
Develop a portfolio that includes specific entries that have been identified by the instructor as indicated below.
1. Required entries (listed on the rubric).
2. Student selected entries (entries you choose related to the objectives and the requirements).
3. Reflective statements concerning the learning activities and how you will use the information and skills gained. (Examples will be provided for you.)

Rubric for Weather Unit Portfolio

Products and Performances	Point Value	Score
Overall organization and appearance	**(10)**	
• The organization and appearance of the portfolio packet.	10	_____
Required entries	**(70)**	
• Essay on how the weather affects me.	5	_____
• Weather instrument assignment.	10	_____
• Weather chart with recorded data for two-week period.	10	_____
• Paper on the effects of weather on people.	10	_____
• Weather map interpretation report.	10	_____
• Diagram of the water cycle.	5	_____
• Lab report on dew point activity.	5	_____
• Lab report on transfer of heat energy.	5	_____
• End of unit essay on how weather affects me.	10	_____
		_____
Student selected entries to complement required entries related to the objectives.	**(10)**	
• Brief description of weather related Web sites. (Example) Current event articles on severe or adverse weather conditions.		_____
Student reflective statements concerning:	**(10)**	
• New knowledge and understandings.	5	_____
• Ideas or plans for using the new information and skills gained.	5	_____
		_____
Total	**100**	_____

CONCEPT MAPS

Science teachers can use concept maps to determine *whether* students are making certain concept connections. They may also use them to determine *how* students are making concept connections at any given time. The teachers may be able to detect misconceptions students have about the information to be learned so they can help students make corrections in their thinking.

Dorough and Rye (1997, 39) also state that concept maps may be used as assessment tools by using the following criteria to assist in developing scoring rubrics.

- ◆ The number of relevant concepts included when the students are expected to complete the maps after "seed" concepts are provided.

- ◆ The number of valid propositions provided by the students to show appropriate relationships among the concepts of the maps.

- ◆ The branching included by students to show links between concepts in the various hierarchies of the maps.

- ◆ The number of appropriate cross-links made by students between the vertical segments of the concept hierarchy.

- ◆ The number of examples of specific concepts provided as examples under concept labels.

Practice is needed to become comfortable with and adept at using concept maps for assessment. The example in Figure 4.7 may be thought of as an assessment exercise where the concept of *momentum* serves as the seed concept.

FIGURE 4.7 CONCEPT MAP

Complete the concept map below to indicate the relationships among the concepts named. In addition to drawing lines to indicate how the concepts can be connected, indicate why you connected them.

```
┌─────────────────────┐
│     Momentum        │
│   (Seed Concept)    │
└─────────────────────┘
```

Concepts to be connected to momentum:

Mass	Time	Weight
Acceleration	Velocity	Distance
Power	Potential Energy	Speed
Impulse	Motion	Force
Work	Kinetic Energy	Gravity
Friction		

Example: Beginning of Student Solution

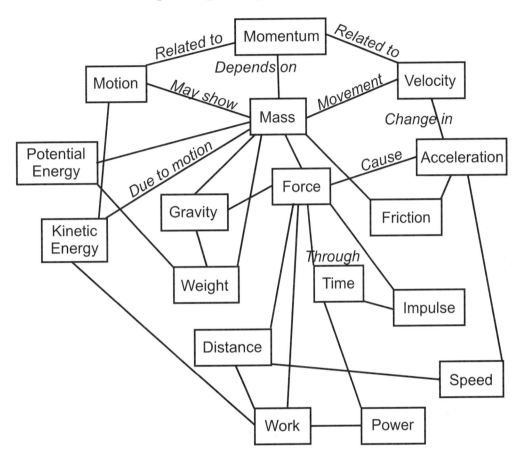

Assessment Rubric for Concept Map

Indicating Level of Understanding of Concept Relationships

*Rating**	*Indicators*
_ 5 _ 4 _ 3 _ 2 _ 1 _ 0	All of the relevant concepts are included.
_ 5 _ 4 _ 3 _ 2 _ 1 _ 0	The concepts are connected to show relationships.
_ 5 _ 4 _ 3 _ 2 _ 1 _ 0	Where relevant, the links show the concepts in the appropriate hierarchy.
_ 5 _ 4 _ 3 _ 2 _ 1 _ 0	The notations and explanations provided to clarify the concept connections are appropriate in number and type.

Total = _____

Comments:

* 5 = Outstanding; 4 = Good; 3 = Adequate; 2 = Poor; 1 = Not Interpretable; 0 = Missing

WRITTEN REPORTS AND RESEARCH PAPERS

When science teachers assign reports and papers for students to complete by applying the knowledge and skills they learned in science class, the tasks can be used as assessments. Students may be required to analyze, synthesize, and manipulate the information learned and apply it in different situations. Teachers can evaluate the written reports and papers in science to determine the students' levels of understanding and their abilities to apply the science concepts learned. To enhance the reliability of the assessments, science teachers should develop scoring criteria and procedures for the products prior to assigning them. See Figure 4.8 for an example of a rubric for a lab report. The criteria and procedures should be shared with students when the assignments are made.

PROJECTS

Science teachers may use projects as assessment tools, in particular, projects that are designed to determine students' abilities to apply science skills and methodologies. Guidelines for project development should be made available to students. Criteria for evaluating the projects should also be developed and communicated to students before the projects are assigned.

Projects used for evaluation purposes are not usually flexible enough to allow the students to choose the topic or problem they pursue. Teachers tend to provide specific parameters for the projects along with the scoring criteria that will be used for assessing the final products in relation to specified objectives. Projects may involve modeling scientific principles or phenomena, completing an experiment or investigation, or developing a product or demonstration.

DEMONSTRATIONS AND EXPERIMENTS

Student demonstrations of science principles and applications enable students to show how well they have mastered science concepts and the procedures for making the demonstration successful. Demonstrations, if done well by students, also require them to understand the information, apply it, and explain related phenomena to other people.

Experiments by students enable the teacher to assess the students' abilities and skills for developing hypotheses, following logical strategies to test the hypotheses, making observations and measurements, making inferences and drawing conclusions, and applying scientific facts and concepts. Experiments done by students can be used to determine how well the students understand scientific methods and concepts and apply them to solve real problems.

FIGURE 4.8 SAMPLE RUBRIC FOR A WRITTEN LAB REPORT

Rating   *Organization of Report*

___ 3   Complete, well organized, and easy to interpret.

___ 2   Contains all required components presented in a logical order.

___ 1   Contains all or some components but lacks a coherent order and clarity.

___ 0   Required components are missing and a clear organization is not evident.

Rating   *Statement of Purpose, Problem, and/or Task*

___ 3   Clearly stated or delineated.

___ 2   Adequately presented for the report.

___ 1   Stated but not clear and/or complete

___ 0   Component not evident.

Rating   *Identification and Appropriateness of Procedures*

___ 3   Very clear and detailed, indicating step-by-step actions.

___ 2   Adequate detail and clarity for repeating procedures.

___ 1   Procedures provided but lack completeness and clarity.

___ 0   Procedures not evident.

Rating   *Pertinent Facts and Results*

___ 3   All pertinent facts and results provided in easy-to-interpret manner.

___ 2   Enough information and results provided to inform problem and/or task.

___ 1   Information concerning results provided but not complete.

___ 0   No results provided.

Rating   *Interpretation (Inferences/Conclusions)*

___ 3   Findings, inferences, and conclusions related to problem/tasks clearly presented.

___ 2   Findings, inferences, and conclusions adequately presented.

___ 1   Findings, inferences, and/or conclusions provided but incomplete.

___ 0   No clear statement of findings or conclusions provided.

Rating   *Overall Presentation (Neatness, Grammatically Correct, etc.)*

___ 3   Report meets presentation standards fully and completely.

___ 2   Report conforms to presentation standards adequately.

___ 1   Report contains some presentation problems.

___ 0   Report includes a large number of errors and mistakes.

Total   Comments:

_____

ORAL REPORTS AND PRESENTATIONS

Student oral presentations concerning projects, demonstrations, and research allow students to verbalize their knowledge and understanding of the related concepts. Students get opportunities to practice and improve their communication skills, but studying the concepts and related explanations for presentation to classmates and the teacher usually require the students to learn the material in greater depth than studying to respond to teacher questions. Students also tend to remember the information longer. See Figure 4.9 for a sample rubric for oral reports.

ORAL INTERVIEWS

Some science teachers may find it helpful to include oral interviews among their assessment strategies. For oral interviews, teachers should speak with individual students in a comfortable nonthreatening atmosphere and ask the students key questions to determine what they know and understand about specific concepts and ideas covered in the instruction. In particular, giving some students the opportunity to express their knowledge and understanding of concepts orally rather than in written form will help the teacher to more accurately assess their performances. These students may be more adept at expressing themselves orally and can provide the teacher with valuable information for adapting future learning activities to their needs.

SELF-REPORTS

Science teachers can have students do self-evaluations and self-assessments in a number of ways that will be motivational for the students and provide helpful information about the students for the teachers. The teachers can then use the information to adapt instruction (for formal assessments) or make decisions about students' achievement and progress. Students may engage in self-assessment activities as components of other assessment methods such as portfolios, journals, interviews, and concept maps. In addition, strategies, procedures, and instruments can be specifically designed for students to directly respond to items or questions concerning their own performances, thoughts, and values. In some cases, the students may be aware of what is being assessed and how the teacher will use the information. In others, students may respond to statements or prompts concerning their feelings, opinions, beliefs, an so forth. without being aware of how the information will be interpreted and used. Science teachers should exercise caution in administering, interpreting, and using student-reported information that is not directly connected to lesson planning or instructing the students in science, especially if students and parents or guardians are not informed about the use of the information.

FIGURE 4.9 SAMPLE RUBRIC: ORAL REPORTS AND PRESENTATIONS

Low High 1 2 3 4 5	Demonstrated Actions
— — — — —	The presenter stood and addressed the class so all could hear and see. Comments:
— — — — —	The appropriate science content was included/covered. Comments:
— — — — —	The content was presented in an appropriate sequence. Comments:
— — — — —	Appropriate descriptions and visuals were provided. Comments:
— — — — —	Information was presented in interesting manner. Comments:
— — — — —	The length of the presentation was appropriate. Comments:
— — — — —	Questions and comments were addressed appropriately. Comments:
Score: _____	

Students can rate themselves using the same criteria and rubrics the teachers have designed for their own use. Science teachers can use questions and items they designed or instruments designed by others to collect student-assessment information. The formats of self-reports and surveys may include Likert-type scales, where students respond to categories such as *strongly agree, agree, undecided, disagree,* and *strongly disagree;* semantic differential formats, which allow rating along a seven-point continuum between a sets of bipolar adjectives; and rating scales.

If self-reports are to be worthwhile, teachers must administer and use them in nonthreatening and supportive environments. Students' honest opinions and ratings are more important than the responses that may be easiest or based on what students think the teacher prefers. See Figure 4.10 for an example of a self-report form.

FIGURE 4.10 EXAMPLE OF A STUDENT SELF-REPORT

Performance in Science

About My Behavior	My Response
I am alert and attentive in science class.	( ) Never ( ) Seldom ( ) Sometimes ( ) Often ( ) Always
I complete and turn in my assignments for science.	( ) Never ( ) Seldom ( ) Sometimes ( ) Often ( ) Always
I make positive contributions to discussions and other activities in science class.	( ) Never ( ) Seldom ( ) Sometimes ( ) Often ( ) Always
I do my share of work as a team member during group activities in science.	( ) Never ( ) Seldom ( ) Sometimes ( ) Often ( ) Always
Most of my science classmates consider me a friend.	( ) Never ( ) Seldom ( ) Sometimes ( ) Often ( ) Always
I am respectful to classmates during discussions and other activities.	( ) Never ( ) Seldom ( ) Sometimes ( ) Often ( ) Always
My work in science class represents the best I can do.	( ) Never ( ) Seldom ( ) Sometimes ( ) Often ( ) Always
Other:	

RUBRICS, RATING FORMS, AND CHECKLISTS

Rubrics are structures or formats used to score student performances and performance products. They usually include the scoring criteria and the numerical values or symbols for indicating the degree to which the student meets the criteria. It is recommended that rubrics and rating forms used for assessments in science be developed after the instructional objectives have been identified, but before the related instruction is provided or the performance tasks are assigned. Going through the development of the assessment criteria and rubrics will assist the teacher in clarifying objectives and providing learning activities that are more focused and appropriate for helping students meet the instructional objectives.

If the criteria, rubrics, and rating forms used for performance assessments are shared with students before instruction, the students will be able to identify the important information and skills to be gained from the lessons and become more focused. The science lessons will become more purposeful, and assessment will be regarded as an integral and important component of the teaching and learning processes. When the students know prior to instruction and assessment what they are expected to accomplish, they have opportunities to do self-assessments and reflections. For many high school students, these opportunities for personal control and responsibility will be empowering and motivating.

Rating forms and checklists are often associated more with the scoring of student performances during direct observations made by the teacher or other scorer (rater). They may be used in rating or checking (1) the presence or absence of some behavior or physical skill such as the proper operation of a piece of equipment, (2) procedures and techniques such as adding solutions in the proper sequence, and (3) aspects of oral reports and presentations such as whether they contained the question or problem statement, the steps followed, and conclusions drawn (see Figure 4.11, p. 130). Checklists may also be used to record aspects of students' behavior such as participation in a group activity (e.g., took notes, made suggestions, operated equipment, reported findings, etc.). See Figure 4.12 (p. 131) for an example of a checklist.

WEB SITES

Here are two useful Web sites for rubrics and other ratings forms:

♦ How to create a rubric

http://7-12educators.about.com/education/7-12educators/library (About.com, Inc., 2000)

♦ Evaluation of self and team members (Davis Honors College, 1997)

http://www-geology.ucdavis.edu/~hnr094/HNR_094_PeerEval.html

FIGURE 4.11 CLASS PARTICIPATION RATING FORM

Score	Ratings & Behavior/Criteria
————	2 Contributes appropriate comments and ideas to class discussions on the course topics. 1 Contributes some information, but sometimes the information is tangential to the topic(s). 0 Never contributes any information or ideas.
————	2 Asks appropriate and relevant questions for information and clarification of concepts. 1 Sometimes asks questions that are off the topic or not relevant to the topic. 0 Never poses relevant questions, problems, or concerns.
————	2 Displays patience, tolerance, and attentiveness when others are talking or expressing different opinions. 1 Is not always respectful and tolerant of others as they present ideas and positions. 0 Shows a dire lack of respect for others in class.
————	2 Participates fully and appropriately in group and class activities but does not cause undue distractions and disruptions. 1 Participates in group and cooperative activities to some extent if encouraged or forced. 0 Resists participation in group and cooperative class activities.
————	2 Shows evidence during class discussions of having read the text and other assigned course materials. 1 Sometimes seems prepared for the class discussions and shows evidence of having read class assignments. 0 Rarely seems prepared or familiar with the assigned reading materials.
————	/10 = Total

FIGURE 4.12 SAMPLE CHECKLIST FOR SETTING UP AND OPERATING TITRATION BURET

Yes ___   No ___   Placed stand on flat surface and securely clamped the buret in place.

Yes ___   No ___   Checked to insure valve is in the "closed" position.

Yes ___   No ___   Filled buret with appropriate indicator 3 to 5 ml above zero volume line.

Yes ___   No ___   Placed empty beaker under tip of buret for adjusting indicator at zero mark.

Yes ___   No ___   Slowly opened buret valve to drip indicator until meniscus reaches zero mark.

Yes ___   No ___   Recorded specific location of the meniscus.

Yes ___   No ___   Removed "waste" beaker and placed test solution under buret tip.

Yes ___   No ___   Opened valve slowly to drip indicator to within about 2 ml of hypothesized value.

Yes ___   No ___   Reduced flow of indicator to single drops for detecting change in beaker solution.

Yes ___   No ___   Noted color change in beaker at appropriate time and closed valve or buret.

Yes ___   No ___   Recorded the final location of the meniscus.

Yes ___   No ___   Flushed buret with distilled water.

Yes ___   No ___   Dismantled and returned all equipment to proper storage areas.

VALIDITY AND RELIABILITY IN ASSESSMENT

Validity and reliability are critical conditions and concepts for science teachers to understand as they relate to measurement, assessment, and evaluation. Whether in block schedules or more traditional schedules, the teachers should be concerned about the accuracy and consistency of tests and other assessment measures they use.

Validity refers to the extent to which the results of a test, performance task (including criteria and standards), or rating accurately reflect what the measure is supposed to assess. If an assessment is valid, then the results will be meaning-ful and appropriate for making inferences and decisions about students' actual performance levels concerning what the assessment was designed to measure. To use an analogy similar to Gronlund's (1998, 23), if we wish to determine how well students can correctly perform tasks (actually solve problems) involving electrical circuits, we may develop two tasks representative of the domain of possible circuitry tasks. If we (a) clearly define the domain of circuitry tasks to be assessed, (b) carefully identify the concepts and skills (behaviors) of the domain, and (c) make sure the two tasks selected or designed clearly represent the concepts and skills included in the domain of circuitry tasks, we are taking steps to ensure assessment validity. Further, if we score or rate students' perfor-mances on the two tasks, we will infer that students with the high scores can do investigations to solve circuitry problems (from the entire domain of possible problems) and do it well. Likewise, we will infer that students receiving low scores will not be able to solve circuitry problems often and/or well. If we go further and infer that students who receive high scores on the two tasks can cor-rectly solve circuitry tasks not included in the original domain of tasks or solve light refraction tasks (problems), it is likely we will be making invalid infer-ences. It is the value or appropriateness of the inferences made that is of concern rather than the actual assessment tasks when validity is questioned.

Classroom assessments should be based on the instructional objectives and on the instruction provided. The assessment results should provide true indica-tions of the students' levels of skills and knowledge (or achievement). A single test or assessment administered by a teacher may not be very valid for the pur-pose for which it is used. If, however, several assessment strategies are used to make the decision or judgment, one would hope that the results across the sev-eral measures will have greater validity. Conceivably, the assessments or grades assigned for student performances over a grading period or semester will not be valid because many of the individual assessments used during the period of time were not valid. In that case, some or all of the students' actual (true) performance or achievement levels will be estimated too low or too high.

Some educators view performance (and alternative) assessments as leading to more valid inferences than traditional assessments because performance tasks are seen as being more directly related to the types of tasks actually taught and to those encountered in real life (being authentic). Gronland (1998, 23) warns, however, that determining validity based on subjective judgments con-cerning relatedness and authenticity can be erroneous and problematic.

Reliability refers to the consistency of the results obtained when the assess-ment is used for the same purpose under the same conditions. For example, if we presented a student with the two circuitry tasks and the student received a score (rating) of 50 out of a possible score of 60, and we presented the student with the same tasks the next day or with two equivalent tasks on the same day, we would expect the student to receive a score close to 50. The consistency of results would indicate that the assessment is relatively free from errors and that we can rely on them for making valid decisions. Assuming no learning between administrations, if the results of two or three administrations of the assessment tasks to the same student vary widely, consistency is lacking and we will have little faith in the information. The inconsistencies can be due to any number of factors. Luck, lack of clarity or understanding, changes in motivation, physical conditions, differences among samples, and perceived expectations are among the variable that can affect performance during assessment. Inconsistencies in judging or rating performance and personal biases of the scorer can also reduce reliability. If an assessment is not considered reliable, it is not considered to be valid either. Therefore, if scores vary widely for the same individual on a particular assessment, we could not expect to draw valid inferences from the results of that assessment. An important goal is to keep the errors that tend to reduce the reliability of assessment results to a minimum. (Gronlund, 1998, 24).

5

TECHNOLOGIES AND TOOLS FOR SCIENCE IN THE BLOCK

The use of technology for instruction involves the application of tools, machines, and materials to implement the processes and activities for meeting instructional aims. Teachers and other educators should apply the available technology, whether it consists of chalk, overhead projectors, or computers, in order to be more effective, more efficient, or both in performing their instructional duties. In today's climate, *instructional technology* is often used to refer to the newer computer-based tools.

Advancements in technology and new devices, programs, and materials are being developed at a fast pace. Consequently, some of the technology and corollary programs and materials become obsolete rather fast. Science teachers need some way of keeping up to date concerning what is available to help them to instruct students, including those who may be exposed in other arenas to the newer technologies for learning or leisure. Technology in the science classroom has two functions: (a) as instructional tools for presenting information, learning tasks and activities, and doing assignments and assessments and (b) as devices for helping to manage and enrich the learning environment efficiently and effectively.

CHOOSING TO USE TECHNOLOGY IN SCIENCE INSTRUCTION

Science teachers should resist the temptation to use or have students use technology simply because it is available. The technology and tools should be selected and used because they serve a purpose in the instruction for developing worthwhile concepts or skills. While it may be advantageous for students to learn to operate a piece of equipment or apply a computer software program, if the skill is not designed to assist the student in learning science content, valuable time needed for the study of science is lost. Purchasing the latest computer equipment before decisions are made concerning the instructional uses of the equipment is not justifiable. It is easy for some educators to get off track and to focus on using technology rather than teaching science. The adage, "the main thing is to keep the main thing the main thing," is appropriate for conveying the importance of using technology to teach science where appropriate and beneficial. Technology skills should not be substituted for science concepts and skills.

In block schedules, technology can be used quite effectively to vary the formats of the instructional activities and enhance student learning and motivation in science. Teachers can use the technologies to help facilitate individualization of instruction by organizing learning centers and stations for students. The experiences designed may allow students to progress at a pace suited to them. The available technologies allow teachers to present information in different ways to accommodate the different learning styles of their students.

The manner in which teachers typically instruct students about the use of a microscope serves as an example of the use of a tool to meet content objectives rather than to teach the operation of the tool itself. In biology classes, teachers usually demonstrate the use or operation of the microscope and then require their students to practice focusing the microscope a few times with the teachers as observers. Teachers rarely plan a long unit covering the operation and various uses of the microscope devoid of teaching science content; rather, they integrate the use of the microscope with teaching the content of the science. The use of the microscope is not taught with the idea that students may need to have more knowledge of microscopes than what is needed for the class activities and the course. In the block, large amounts of time can be consumed while students manipulate materials and equipment, leaving less time to cover science and use science processes. Therefore, it is important to integrate the use of technology into the teaching of science rather than merely teach technology use in the science classroom and during the block of time scheduled for science instruction.

In *Benchmarks for Science Literacy*, the American Association for the Advancement of Science (AAAS, 1993) challenges science teachers to "build technology education into the curriculum, as well as to use technology to promote learning, so that all students become well informed about the nature, power, and limitations of technology." Because of advances in technology, it is now possible to get the most up-to-date information on science topics. That was not the case two decades ago. In the 1970s, biotechnology was a growing field and new information in the field was generated rapidly. Yet, little of that information reached teachers and students at the secondary level. They primarily depended on textbooks that were usually several years in production and adoption. Developments and information concerning restriction endonucleases, plasmids, and recombinant DNA occurred, but were not readily available to students. Now, the availability of computers, CD-ROM databases, and numerous Internet sites enable teachers and students have access to recent discoveries and information in the field of science. These technologies and their availability allow science teachers to safely and efficiently demonstrate potentially dangerous laboratory experiments and to take students on electronic field trips to exotic places.

The following are some general guidelines to consider in selecting or choosing technology and materials for teaching science.

- Is the cost consistent with the amount of use that will be made of them?

- How soon will the item or its use become obsolete?

- Can the identified concepts and/or skills be taught more effectively and/or efficiently than in any other way?

- Is there adequate room for storage or safekeeping when not in use?

- Will students be able to use the materials or are they for demonstration or record keeping only?

- Will the item(s) support instruction in other areas of the curriculum?

- Will the item(s) support the adopted instructional philosophy and desired approach (e.g., a constructivist and inquiry-oriented approach)?

COMPUTERS AND OTHER DEVICES

Some phenomena and theoretical models that are described or used in science classes can be simulated and visually represented by computers. Visual representations and images of abstract, complex, and unobservable relationships can be provided for students to help them think about and develop conceptual understandings they would find impossible without such assistance. For example, the structure of molecules can be represented and manipulated to depict their interactions with other molecules in a chemical reaction or the behavior of sound waves can be simulated through a computer program for physics students.

The use of a computer to instruct students concerning the content of a unit or course is called *computer-assisted instruction* (CAI). CAI can take many forms, including drill and practice, simulations, tutorials, problem solving, testing or assessing concepts and skills, information gathering and research, and communications or exchange of ideas and information. Squires and McDougall (1994, 62) refer to five types of student–computer-assisted learning interactions: recognition, recall, reconstructive understanding or comprehension, global reconstructive or intuitive understanding, and constructive understanding.

The different types of CAI activities may allow the students to exercise different amounts of control as they participate in the activities. Squires and McDougall (1994, 57–64) caution users, however, about trying to place software and programs in distinct and exclusive categories because of the range of designs and uses possible. Drill-and-practice activities enable students to repeat coverage of information or practice actions and activities that may require rote learning or skill development. Computer programs that provide simulations are popular in science instruction, especially if the programs are interactive, so that students can provide input and determine the effects of their actions. Such interactive simulations not only help with learning the concepts but increases student motivation. Tutorial programs consist of activities or question-and-answer formats to help students master some particular body of content and/or skills for a particular purpose. Computer software is available that will allow simulations of phenomena such as specific weather conditions, volcanic eruptions, airplane flight, and blood flow in the human body. In chemistry, students can see and study the effects of combining chemicals in a relatively short period of time and without fear of explosions, the presence of noxious fumes, and spills. In biology, students can use interactive videodiscs to perform dissections. In physics, students can observe the effects of different objects colliding with other objects having different mass and traveling at different velocities. A teacher-made tutorial can be designed to assist students who were absent from class or who need the extra exposure to fully understand the content. This is important for classes in the block because when students miss a class session, they may miss a large amount of content coverage. Programs that present problems to be solved by the student or groups of students tend to be interactive and afford students various response options. The students proceed through the program based on their responses until they solve the problem and receive scores or ratings based on their responses (the actions chosen). Most teachers and students now have access to computers for obtaining information available locally as well as what is available nationally and globally. Students can visit Websites related to science topics of interest and select and gather the information desired. Students and teachers can also locate the e-mail addresses for and communicate with scientists and others who may have expertise and/ or interests in a particular topic. Descriptive statistics, mathematical models, and graphs of collected information can be calculated or developed in seconds by the computer. This allows variables in investigations to be changed and recalculated quickly.

Sensors and probes that can be connected to microcomputers are now available commercially and can be used in science for collecting data on physical phenomena in real time and recording or displaying the results. Computer interfaces are available that have pH meters (to measure the acidity of solutions) and sensors for temperature, pressure, oxygen, and other variables. Environmental conditions and variables, including temperature, humidity, atmospheric pressure, wind speed, sound, light intensity, and motion, can also be measured. Other sensors can measure heart rate, blood pressure, and other changes in human and other organisms. Students and teachers can use the computer-based sensing devices for a variety of demonstrations, investigations, and projects. Science teachers may also have occasion to use or have students use graphing calculators to help solve problems or to develop concepts in science. Digital cameras are valuable for developing pictures or images to develop slide shows and presentations of local phenomena and events.

Vernier Software Company in Portland, Oregon, assembles and sells a variety of probes that are useful for data collection in science education. David Vernier, the founder and former physics teacher, started developing probeware for educational purposes in his garage. Based on the authors' experiences, the company is user friendly for science teachers and provides ample technical support. The Web site for the company is www.vernier.com. The mailing address is: Vernier Software & Technology, 13979 SW Millikan Way, Beaverton, OR 97005-

2886. The following are some of the probes available from Vernier Software Company:

- 3-Axis Accelerometer
- 25-g Accelerometer
- Barometer
- Biology Gas Pressure Sensor
- CO_2 Gas Sensor
- Colorimeter
- Conductivity Probe
- Current & Voltage Probe System
- Digital Control Unit
- Direct-Connect Temperature Probe
- Dissolved Oxygen Probe
- Dual-Range Force Sensor
- EKG Sensor
- Exercise Heart Rate Monitor
- Extra-Long Temperature Probe
- Flow Rate Sensor
- Gas Pressure Sensor
- Heart Rate Monitor
- Instrumentation Amplifier
- Ammonium Ion-Selective Electrode
- Calcium Ion-Selective Electrode
- Chloride Ion-Selective Electrode
- Nitrate Ion-Selective Electrode
- Light Sensor
- Magnetic Field Sensor
- Microphone
- Motion Detector
- O_2 Gas Sensor
- pH Sensor
- Pressure Sensor
- Radiation Monitor
- Relative Humidity Sensor
- Respiration Monitor Belt
- Rotary Motion Sensor
- Stainless Steel Temperature Probe
- Student Force Sensor
- Student Radiation Monitor
- Turbidity Sensor
- Thermocouple
- Vernier Photogate
- Voltage Probe
- Water Depth Sampler

A versatile and reasonably priced computer microscope is available from Intel Play. Visit the Web site at http://intelplay.com (Intel Corporation, 1999). As with other computer technologies, teachers should get information on the computer system requirements for operating the microscope and ensure that a computer is available with the specifications and capacity to operate the microscope program.

In cases in which actual science investigations and experiments may be too time-consuming, expensive, dangerous, or controversial, videodiscs and computer-based virtual labs and simulations provide highly effective, alternative activities for students. Some microcomputer environments will allow students to make hypotheses, test them, observe the results, and come to conclusions. Students can input into a computer program the information to represent the concrete materials or select from options given, and the computer will generate and display the results. This can be done in significantly less time than is required for the actual experiments. Videodiscs can be used to help students make connections between classroom lessons presented in other modes and events and activities outside the classroom. Teachers and students may be able to freeze-frame steps in videodisc presentations or view the actions in slow motion for better observation and understanding. Teachers can organize a large number of clips and pictures in a short amount of time to form lessons or presentations.

COMPUTER SOFTWARE

Science teachers should be directly involved in the selection of the computer software they will use for instruction. It is expected that technology specialists and other school personnel serve as members of a software selection team, but the teachers' input should carry significant weight because they will be the primary users who must integrate the software with the other instructional materials. The science teachers should review and evaluate software for content, purpose, and appropriateness for integration with their teaching approaches.

Teachers can determine what computer software is available for science instruction by contacting publishing companies, educational and professional organizations, and software distributors. Teachers may also locate software information in journals, magazines, and other publications. The descriptive information may provide important information for making decisions about requesting software for preview purposes. The best way to determine if a piece of software is suitable for the purpose intended is to preview or test it prior to securing it for use with students.

The criteria provided in Figure 5.1 for the review and evaluation of computer software in science were adapted from sets of criteria (MicroSIFT Courseware Evaluation Form and Blease's Educational Software Selection Criteria) reported by Squires and McDougall (1994, 34–37).

MULTIMEDIA APPLICATIONS

Science teachers can combine the use of media and materials in ways that will make their teaching effective and exciting. The different media can be used to present information or activities in sequence or simultaneously to complement one another. The essential ingredient in using the various media tools effectively is that they support or reinforce each other for enhancing the instruction. For example, the teacher may wish to show a picture or image of an organism using one medium, present an audio of the sounds the organism makes in its natural habitat using another medium, and show the physical features of the natural environment using a third medium, all simultaneously.

Multimedia applications in the science classroom offer many opportunities for motivating and actively involving students in their learning. Interactive multimedia allows students to learn in a variety of ways, including seeing,

FIGURE 5.1 SOFTWARE REVIEW AND EVALUATION CRITERIA

Rating Scale

0 = Evidence totally lacking   3 = Highly evident

1 = Some evidence   4 = Superior concerning the quality

2 = Adequate evidence

Content Criteria   Total _____

1. Is the content accurate?   _____

2. Is the content directly related to the adopted science   _____
    curriculum?

3. Is the content free of race, ethnic, sex, and other ste- _____
    reotypes?

4. Is the content appropriate for the intended age/grade   _____
    level?

5. Are the purpose and objectives of the materials evi-   _____
    dent and appropriate?

6. Are appropriate supplementary materials provided   _____
    with the program?

Presentation Criteria   Total
                                                          _____

1. Does the presentation follow a logical sequence?   _____

2. Is the presentation of the information clear and easy   _____
    to understand?

3. Is the content presented in an interesting and stimu-   _____
    lating manner?

4. Is the age/developmental level(s) identified for which _____
    the program is suited?

5. Are the presentation qualities (graphics, color, sound, _____
    etc.) adequate?

6. Does the program allow flexibility of presentation   _____
    (pause, alternative sequences, etc.)?

7. Is the presentation of information/activities provided _____
    in a manner consistent with the educational philoso-
    phy employed in instruction?

Operation Criteria	*Total* _____
1. Are the operating instructions clear?	_____
2. Are the hardware requirements made explicit?	_____
3. Is the program easy to start and operate?	_____
4. Are program control and input features easy to understand and apply?	_____
5. Are the materials for user support and help effective?	_____
6. Can the program be operated adequately on the available computer hardware?	_____
7. Can the learner control the rate and sequence of the presentation?	_____
8. Does the program generate useful information (feedback) for the teacher concerning student responses?	_____
9. Is the program reliable under normal use?	_____
10. Can input changes and error corrections be made easily?	_____

reading, writing, hearing, and doing. Through such applications, science teachers can accommodate the learning modalities and styles of the diverse student groups that compose most classes. The use of multimedia presentations can enable science teachers to reach more students more of the time. Learning activities and presentations that include a variety of reality-based objects and computer-generated images increase the potential that science teachers can effectively meet the needs of and teach science content to a variety of students whether varied based on cultural backgrounds, learning styles, abilities, or interests.

Teachers can use commercially available multimedia packages and other materials and presentations along with materials and presentations they or their students develop to make lessons relevant and exciting for the students. Videodiscs and CD-ROMs are commercially available that contain images, captions, and sounds relevant to a variety of topics in science. Videodiscs provide information in visual formats that allow students to develop rich mental models and to recognize patterns for interpreting information and problems. The information on the videodisc and the interactive nature of computer programs and authoring systems enable teachers and students to choose information from sources to customize their presentation to fit their purposes. For teachers who plan to incorporate the use of presentation software to design and customize the content of their lessons, Duet (1999, 4) provides some suggestions for enhancing the chances of presenting information with the desired results. First, Duet points out that the slides or visuals should be legible and uncluttered, and the equipment (hardware) should be checked to make certain it is functional. Second, the presentation should be designed so the students do not have to search around the screen to locate the relevant information. Other suggestions include:

- Use cool colors (blues and greens) for backgrounds.
- Add visual movement by using gradations and background.
- Use bright contrasting colors like yellow, yellow-orange or white for text.
- Keep bullet points short; use phrases, not sentences.
- Be consistent with your design or template.

THE INTERNET

The World Wide Web (WWW) makes a vast amount of science information and curricular materials available to students and teachers. There are numerous science and science education sites available. The Internet provides a source of instructional activities, lesson plans, and curricular materials. A resource handbook called *Making the Best Use of the Internet to Enhance Science Instruction (Grades 6–12)*, by Sarah DiRuscio (1998), provides valuable ideas and Internet sites. See http://www.4forefront.com (Forefront Curriculum, 2000).

Of course, there are many resources and sites on the World Wide Web that can be distracting or of little or no value to teachers and students. Students, in particular, may need some assistance and guidance to evaluate sites and sources to use for educational purposes. Jacobson and Cohen (1997, 4) list four questions they believe to be important for students to consider in assessing a Web site for valid information concerning a topic:

1. Who provided and posted the information? At first glance a Web site may seem creditable but further investigations may reveal otherwise.

2. What authority or special knowledge does the author have?

3. Does the site exhibit a bias or slant? Addressing this question may require extra time to do a critical assessment.

4. When was the site last updated? Addressing this question reveals whether the site is being maintained.

Jacobson and Cohen (1997, 4) also provide a list of key criteria for students to use to evaluate Internet sites. The criteria concerns the four general areas of:

1. *Purpose:* Try to determine why the site was created. Was it designed to sell something, to persuade, to inform, etc.?

2. *Source:* Identify the source of the site. Who are the sponsoring individuals or entities and are e-mail links provided to allow questions and comments concerning the site?

3. *Content:* Determine if the site is valid for the purpose desired?

    a. Check for accuracy: Because Web sites are not usually refereed or reviewed check for identification of original source information and documentation of sources.

    b. Check for comprehensiveness: Assess the depth and scope of coverage.

    c. Check for currency: Determine if the site has been updated recently.

    d. Check for hyperlinks: Check for links that are relevant and appropriate and do not assume those given are the most appropriate available.

4. *Style and Functionality:* A site that is designed well and presented in an appropriate writing style is usually easy to navigate and provides better information.

Science teachers should provide detailed guidelines and roles for students for using the available technology in the classroom. This is especially important when allowing students to use the Internet for communicating with others as a part of the planned learning experiences and for locating and accessing information. Teachers and students should adhere to acceptable ethical standards in sending, retrieving, and using information and messages. Students should receive instruction and guidelines concerning the ethics of Internet usage and copyright laws before they are allowed to use the Internet. Several school districts in Virginia have developed guidelines and acceptable use agreements for students and their parents to read and sign prior to giving the students access to the Internet and the school equipment and network. The student guidelines for use of the Internet and electronic mail and the acceptable use agreement statements in Figure 5.2 are adapted from the *Harrisonburg High School and Harrisonburg City Schools 1999–2000 Student and Parent Handbook* (Harrisonburg High School, 1999, 35–37) in Virginia.

FIGURE 5.2 STUDENT GUIDELINES FOR USE
OF THE INTERNET AND ELECTRONIC MAIL

- ◆ Personal Safety and Privacy
  - Do not post personal contact information about yourself or other people. This includes name, address, telephone number, school address, work address, etc.
  - Do not agree to meet with anyone you have communicated with on-line, unless accompanied by your parent or legal guardian.
  - Do not repost or forward a message that was sent privately to you without permission from the person who originally sent the message.
  - Do not post private information about another person.
  - Report to a teacher or appropriate school administrator any activity that you believe is inappropriate, offensive, or makes you uncomfortable.
- ◆ Illegal Activities
  - Do not attempt to gain unauthorized access to any computer system or go beyond personal authorized access. This includes logging into the system through another person's account or accessing another person's file.
  - Do not attempt to disrupt the computer system or destroy data by spreading computer viruses or by other means.
  - Do not use the system to engage in any illegal act, such as arranging for drug sale, purchasing alcohol, threatening another person, etc.
- ◆ System Security
  - Assume responsibility for your individual account and take precautions to prevent others from using your account. Do not reveal your password to another person.
  - Notify a teacher or administrator of any possible security problems with the system.
  - Follow computer virus protection procedures when downloading software.
- ◆ Acceptable Language
  - Do not use inappropriate language in any public or private messages or in material posted on Web pages.
  - Do not use obscene, profane, lewd, inflammatory, threatening or disrespectful language in communications.
  - Do not engage in personal attacks, including prejudicial or discriminatory attacks.

- Do not harass another person or persistently act in a manner that annoys another person.
- Do not post false or defamatory information about a person or organization.

♦ Respecting Resource Limits
- Do not download large files unless absolutely necessary.
- Do not post chain letters or send a message to large numbers of people.
- Check your electronic mail frequently and delete unwanted messages promptly.

♦ Plagiarism and Copyright Infringement
- Do not plagiarize works or information found on the Internet. Plagiarism is taking the ideas or writings or others and presenting them as if they were your own.
- Respect the rights of copyright owners. If you are unsure whether a work is copyrighted or whether you may reproduce a certain work, consult with your teacher before using it.

♦ Inappropriate Access
- Do not use the system to access material that is obscene (pornographic), advocates illegal acts, or advocates violence and harm to other people.
- Check with your parent or guardian when in doubt about accessing and/or communicating via the Internet and electronic mail.

Internet Acceptable Use Agreement Form

As a user of the school computer network, I hereby agree to comply with the rules stated in the *Acceptable Use Agreement* for communicating over the network in a responsible manner while honoring all relevant laws and restrictions. Should I commit any violation knowingly, my access privileges may be revoked and school disciplinary actions and/or appropriate legal actions may be taken.

Student Signature: _____ Date: _____

As a parent or legal guardian of the minor signed above, I have read the *Acceptable Use Agreement*. I understand that this access is designed for educational purposes and that the school district has taken precaution to eliminate controversial material. I also recognize, however, that it is impossible for the school district personnel to restrict access to all controversial materials. I will not hold the school district responsible for materials acquired on the network. Further, I accept full responsibility for supervision if and when my child's use is not in a school setting.

I hereby give the (appropriate name) school district permission to issue an account for my child, and I certify that the information contained on this form is true and correct.

Parent (or Guardian) Signature: _____ Date: _____

Students will not be permitted access to the Internet until this form is signed and returned. It is the responsibility of the parent/guardian to inform the school if the status of this agreement changes.

Students and teachers can use electronic mail to communicate with each other and with scientists throughout the country and the world concerning topics of interest. This potentially valuable learning medium should be used properly, with ample consideration and respect for other people.

SOME WEB SITES

♦ www.awesomelibrary.org/science.html *or* www.neat-schoolhouse.org/science.html (EDI and R. Jerry Adams, 1996)

♦ ww.enc.org/focus/topics/inquiry (Eisenhower National Clearinghouse)

See the Appendix for other Web sites.

RECORDING AND MANAGING INFORMATION

Using the computer to help create files, store information, compile records of students' progress, track other resources or keep inventory, and develop reports is referred to as *computer-assisted management* (CAM). Once science teachers get the computer hardware and software they need, using the computer for management purposes (the recording, maintenance, and retrieval of records) can become relatively easy and convenient. Maintaining class rolls, keeping records of attendance and other student data, recording and calculating course grades, maintaining equipment inventories, and keeping pacing guides are among the many uses for computers and computer software. Of course, keeping the information up to date is still time-consuming because the appropriate commands must be given and entries must be made.

Science teachers who provide instruction in the block find computers very helpful and for managing time effectively and efficiently. The teachers can record, compile, manage, and retrieve information concerning students' achievement, opinions, and behaviors and concerning materials and equipment. Then, they can provide the appropriate commands to organize the information and generate summaries and compilations of the information. Computer programs for recording and managing student attendance and assessment information, grades, and the like have become very *user friendly* for teachers.

Most teachers use computers to do word processing for writing lesson plans, providing directions and information for students, and developing assessment tests and tasks for students. The available computer programs enable teachers to make changes, deletions, and additions to the information and documents with ease. Information can be moved around, reordered, copied, and merged with other information. Many word-processing programs include spreadsheet and graphics features, and the products of those operations can be integrated into text documents. The information can be edited, copied, and printed with ease at any time. Some programs include features for reordering or sequencing information based on identified criteria or commands after the information has been entered.

Additionally, programs are available for developing, storing, and retrieving test items and generating tests to meet specified criteria. Tests can also be administered and scored by computer. Web sites that have test development and related features include:

- http://company.blackboard.net/Bb (Blackboard, Inc., 1999)
- http://quizlab2.funbrain.com/cgi-bin (FunBrain.com, LLC, 1997–2000)
- http://medlib.med.utah.edu/hw/ (Sharon Dennis, Spencer S. Eccles Health Sciences Library, University of Utah, 1998)

TECHNOLOGY SKILLS FOR SCIENCE TEACHERS

Science teachers should be able to perform the following activities to adequately utilize available technology in the classroom:

- Connect and operate computers and peripheral (ancillary) hardware and equipment, including printers and scanners
- Possess basic knowledge of and the ability to use a basic vocabulary for communicating with others concerning computer and other instructional technologies
- Operate a computer to produce printed documents for science instruction
- Use the computer to send and receive information and messages electronically (including accessing the Internet and communicating via e-mail)
- Identify, locate, and evaluate technology hardware and software to use in instruction
- Use search strategies to retrieve information for CD-ROMs and videodiscs
- Use computers and other technologies to collect, record, organize, and manage data and information (including using spreadsheet, graphics, and statistical programs)

♦ Integrate databases, graphics, and spreadsheets into word-processed documents on a computer

♦ Use probeware or sensor devices, digital cameras, scanners, video projection equipment, and other devices in connection with a computer too enhance instruction for students in science

♦ Access and use presentation packages and programs to develop effective instructional presentations and activities

♦ Integrate the use of computers and other commonly available technologies into instructional plans, activities, and assignments for students

♦ Apply various technologies in interactive and integrated ways to meet the needs of diverse learners in a variety of educational settings (including making multimedia presentations concerning science topics)

♦ Develop and maintain a Website or "home page" document that can be assessed by worldwide networks

♦ Possess and apply knowledge of ethical and legal issues to avoid problems related to the use of technology and information available through the use of technology

TEXTBOOKS

Textbooks and the accompanying resources provided by publishing companies continue to be key resources for students and teachers in the sciences. The text materials serve many functions for science courses depending upon the students, teachers, and schools. In some cases, the textbook serves to describe the curriculum relative to the content and methodologies included. In other cases, the text is considered to be one of the resources from which the student and teacher may draw information and activities in the teaching and learning processes.

Because many teachers depend on textbooks as the primary sources of information and learning activities, textbooks and their corollary materials for science should be selected with care. Often textbooks contain information that is too broad in scope and presented in an encyclopedia form. The coverage may be superficial or cursory, providing little basis for developing student interest and understanding. Inadequate textbooks selected and used by text-dependent teachers may contribute to the negative views many students develop about science and science education. Textbooks in science should be viewed and used as resources and references rather than as curriculum guides and the only sources of information for students.

Carefully selected science textbooks can be very useful tools in the teaching and learning processes for curriculum planners, teachers, parents, and, of course, students. Whether the texts are used as guides in the curriculum, references, or courses of study, ample consideration should be given to the selection of the texts to serve the appropriate purposes for which they are adopted. Some states and school districts have recently included the selection of multimedia science programs and software packages among the resources adopted for courses or curriculum components.

The textbook selection process may differ depending upon the state, district, and school. In many instances, teachers are directly involved in the selection process, either in making initial recommendations or in choosing from a list of texts identified by others. The teachers usually serve on selection committees that have representation from other groups such as school administrators, parents, and interested citizens.

Listed in Figure 5.3 are criteria that were complied by a science methods class after reviewing available science textbooks and brainstorming as a group. Any of the criteria considered important to textbook reviewers can be used with a rating scale for comparing competing text materials.

It is important that teachers model the appropriate use of textbook materials by students. Science teachers may demonstrate that adopted texts are sources of information and structure for science classes but students still need to think for themselves and question or retain a certain amount of healthy skepticism about the text and other sources of information. Teachers and students will find it valuable and informative to consult a variety of sources to secure information, answers, and ideas concerning a topic. Textbook materials should not be considered the only and final authority for science information. Therefore, the science teacher should require students to use the library, various multimedia, and on-line resources to access information concerning the course content.

Scientific journals, periodicals, newspapers, magazines, trade books, and the World Wide Web are other resources that science teachers and students can use to validate, supplement, and complement information found in the textbook materials. In cases where the textbook materials are found to be inappropriate, teacher may wish to substitute other materials altogether. However, teachers should be cautious about straying too far from the prescribed curriculum relative to content and process. Maps, globes, charts, graphs, and pictures are other useful tools for science instruction. Teachers who plan well and implement lessons adapted for their students usually gain access to a variety of primary source materials and significantly reduce their reliance on textbooks.

The sets of textbook materials available to science teachers typically contain more information or cover a broader scope of content than can be included in a course in the manner prescribed by many science education authorities. Therefore, science teachers need to plan, sequence, and teach science lessons and units to help students accomplish objectives identified. The development of pacing guides to use along with other strategies mentioned earlier in this volume can help with tasks. The American Association for the Advancement of Science (AAAS, 1990) and other sources have emphasized the importance of teaching a few concepts well rather than covering a wide scope of content that will not be retained by students.

FIGURE 5.3 TEXT REVIEW AND EVALUATION CRITERIA

Rating Scale

0 = Evidence totally lacking   3 = Highly evident

1 = Some evidence   4 = Superior concerning the quality

2 = Adequate evidence

General Criteria   Total _____

Are the authors and publisher available for questions and comments?   _____

Are the materials up to date and accurate?   _____

Are the materials attractive and inviting in appearance?   _____

Are the philosophical and developmental approaches employed discernible and appropriate?   _____

Presentation Criteria   Total _____

Is the reading level of the material appropriate?   _____

Is the content difficulty level appropriate?   _____

Are the materials interesting to read?   _____

Is the print material easy to read (legible with appropriate print size, line spacing, illustrations, etc.)?   _____

Are there "normal" vocabulary connections to the "foreign language" of science?   _____

Are there enough pictures, diagrams, tables, figures, etc., to complement the print materials?   _____

Are visuals (pictures, charts, graphs, etc.) well done and appropriate (i.e., "real life" pictures, colors used in charts to aid in interpretation)?   _____

Is there enough variety in the way the content is presented?   _____

Are the end-of-chapter reviews and summaries analytical and scientific?   _____

Is the information presented in a logical sequence?   _____

Is the information organized so that concepts build upon previously learned information (i.e., early chapters lay the foundation for later chapters)?   _____

Is the format for chapters or sections "user friendly" for students?   _____

Is the information presented without bias and based on proven scientific information (especially when covering evolution)?   _____

Do the materials allow for accommodating diverse student groups?   _____

Are accommodations made for students who speak English as a second language (i.e., English, Spanish, and French glossaries)?   _____

Do the materials allow for flexibility in teaching and learning styles and approaches?   _____

Do the materials make provisions for employing a discovery approach to teaching?   _____

Do the materials allow for investigation and experimentation by the student?   _____

Is there emphasis on developing broad understandings and concepts rather than on learning detailed facts?   _____

Is there emphasis on the development of science process skills (i.e., measuring, predicting, hypothesizing, interpreting data, etc.)?   _____

Do the materials enable the development of a historical perspective?   _____

Do the materials promote the development of problem-solving skills?   _____

Content Criteria   Total _____

Is there enough detail and thorough coverage of the information?   _____

Do the chapter introductions have enough detail to get students excited about the topic?   _____

Do the materials include enough coverage of environmental concepts and information?   _____

Do the materials include adequate coverage (inclusion) of multicultural aspects?   _____

Do the materials cover all of the areas of science pertinent to the course? (List those areas not covered.)   _____

Is the degree of consistency between the materials (content), the (local) school curriculum, and other guidelines (i.e., state level) adequate?   _____

Do the text materials provide information for further research by students?   _____

Are additional reading lists included for students?   _____

Does the text have little sections aside showing relevant information that can help clarify material and show interesting side topics?   _____

Are adequate supplementary materials and media included (transparencies, test banks, videodisc, CD-ROM, etc.)?   _____

Does the text summarize the information enough to clarify without making the summaries enough for the student to "go by" (use exclusively) for the tests?   _____

Are adequate and practical questions provided in appropriate places for the students to study and review?   _____

Is the table of contents complete and directive?   _____

Is the glossary comprehensive and easy to use?   _____

Is the index complete and helpful in locating content?   _____

REFERENCES

ARTICLES AND BOOKS

AAAS (American Association for the Advancement of Science)(1993). *Benchmarks for Science Literacy*. New York: Oxford University Press.

AAAS (American Association for the Advancement of Science) (1990). *Science for All Americans*. New York: Oxford University Press.

Arendt, J. D. (1970). New scheduling patterns and the foreign language teacher. *ERIC Focus Reports on the Teaching of Foreign Languages*, Number 18. [ED 043 269] 18pp.

Ball, W. H., & Brewer, P. F. (1996). In R. L. Canady & M. D. Rettig, *Teaching in the Block* (pp. 29–64). Larchmont, NY: Eye On Education.

Bloom, B. S., Engelhart, M. D., Furst, E. J., Hill, W. H., & Krathwohl, D. R. (1956). *Taxonomy of Educational Objectives: Handbook I: Cognitive Domain*. New York: David McKay.

Canady, R. L., & Rettig, M.D. (1995). *Block Scheduling: A Catalyst for Change in High Schools.*. Princeton, N.J.: Eye On Education Digest.

Canady, R. L., & Rettig, M. D. (1996). *Teaching in the Block*. Larchmont, NY: Eye On Education.

Clough, D. B., James, T. L., & Witcher, A. E. (1996, September). Curriculum mapping and instructional supervision. *NASSP Bulletin, 80(581)*, 79–82.

Cothron, J. H., Giese, R. N., & Rezba, R. J. (1993). *Students and Research: Practical Strategies for Science Classrooms and Competitions* (2nd ed.). Dubuque, Iowa: Kendal/Hunt Publishing Company.

Day, M. M., Ivanov, C. P., & Binkley, S. (1996). Tackling block scheduling. *The Science Teacher, 63(6)*, 25–27.

DiRuscio, S. (1998). *Making the Best Use of the Internet to Enhance Science Instruction (Grades 6–12)*. Bellevue, WA: Bureau of Education & Research.

Dorough, D. K., & Rye, J. A. (1997). Mapping for understanding. *The Science Teacher, 64(1)*, 37–41.

Duet, R (1999). Presentations that work. *Acumen, 1(1)*, 4.

Ellington, H., Addinall, E., & Percival, F. (1981). *Games and Simulations in Science Education*. New York: Nichols Publishing Company.

Glynn, S. (1997). Drawing mental models. *The Science Teacher. 64(1,)* 30–32.

Gronlund, N. E. (1998). *Assessment of Student Achievement* (6th ed.), Boston: Allyn and Bacon.

Gunter, M. A., Estes, T., & Schwab, J. (1995). *Instruction: A Models Approach*. Needham Heights, MA: Simon and Schuster.

Harrison, A. G. (1998). Modelling in science lessons: Are there better ways to learn with models? *School Science and Mathematics, 98*(8), 420–429.

Harrisonburg High School (1999). *Harrisonburg High School and Harrisonburg City Schools 1999–2000 Student/Parent Handbook.* Harrisonburg, VA.

Hassard, J. (1992). *Minds on Science: Middle and Secondary School Methods.* New York: HarperCollins.

Hunter, M. (1982). *Mastery Teaching.* El Segundo, CA: TIP Publications.

Jacobs, H. H. (1997). *Mapping the Big Picture: Integrating Curriculum and Assessment K–12.* Alexandria, VA: Association for Supervision and Curriculum Development.

Jacobson, T. E., & Cohen, L. B. (1997). Teaching students to evaluate Internet sites. *The Teaching Professor, 11*(7), 4.

Johnson, S. C. (1972). Flexible-modular scheduling. *Educational Management Series Number 4* [ED 061 580], 10pp.

Kubiszyn, T., & Borich, G. (2000). *Educational Testing and Measurement: Classroom Application and Practice, 6th ed.* New York: John Wiley & Sons.

Lawson, A. E. (1995). *Science Teaching and the Development of Thinking.* Belmont, CA:Wadsworth Publishing Company.

Lyons, P. (1992). *Thirty-Five Lesson Formats: A Sourcebook of Instructional Alternatives.* Englewood Cliffs, NJ: Educational Technology Publications.

Morie, E. D. (1996). Simulations. In R. L. Canady & M. D.Rettig, *Teaching in the Block* (pp. 141–162). Larchmont, NY: Eye On Education.

National Research Council (1996). *National Science Education Standards.* Washington, DC: National Academy Press.

Pettus, A. M. (1998). Bathymetric mapping: Making underwater profile charts. *Science Activities, 35*(3), 24–27.

Pheeney, P. (1998). A portfolio primer. *The Science Teacher, 65*(7), 36–39.

Rudner, L. M., & Boston, C. (1994). Performance assessment. *The ERIC Review (winter) 3*(1), 2–11.

Ruiz-Primo, M. A., & Shavelson, R. J. (1996). Rhetoric and reality in science performance assessment: An update. *Journal of Research in Science Teaching, 33*(10), 1045–1063.

Sharan, S., Shachar, H., & Levine, T. (1999). *The Innovative School: Organization and Instruction.* Westport, CT: Bergin & Garvey.

Squires, D., & McDougall, A. (1994). *Choosing and Using Educational Software: A Teachers' Guide.* Washington, DC: The Falmer Press.

Tobin, K. G., & Capie, W. (1981) Wait-time and learning in science (ATE Outstanding Paper for 1981). Burlington,NC: Carolina Biological Supply Company. pp. 1–10.

Trowbridge, L. W., Bybee, R. W., & Powell, J. C. (2000). *Teaching Secondary School Science: Strategies for Developing Science Literacy, 7th ed.* Upper Saddle River, NJ: Prentice-Hall.

vos Savant, M. (2000, April 30). Ask Marilyn. *Parade Magazine,* p. 15.

Wise, K., & Okey, J. (1983). A meta-analysis of the effects of various science teaching strategies on achievement. *Journal of Research in Science Teaching, 20*(5), 434.

WEB SITES

About.com, Inc. (2000). How to Create a Rubric. http://7-12educators.about.com/education/7-12educators/library

Blackboard.com, Blackboard Inc. (1999). http://company.blackboard.net/Bb

Center for the Study of Classroom Processes (2000). http://artsci-ccwin.concordia.ca/education/cscp/Try_1.htm

Davis Honors College (1997). Evaluation of Self and Team Members, http://www-geology.ucdavis.edu/~hnr094/HNR_094_PeerEval.html

Discovery Communications, Inc. (1999). http://puzzlemaker.school.discovery.com/

EDI and Dr. Jerry Adams (1996–2000). www.awesomelibrary.org/science.html

Eisenhower National Clearinghouse (2000). www.enc.org/focus/tpics/inquiry

Flinn Scientific (2000). http://www.flinnsci.com.

Forefront Curriculum (2000). http://www.4front.com

Funbrain.com, FunBrain.com, LLC (1997–2000). http://quizlab2.funbrain.com/

Intel Corporation (1999), Intel.Play, http://intelplay.com

Optimizing National Education, Inc., (1998). http://.opnated.org/

Peter Ommundsen, 1999. Critical Thinking in Biology: Case Problems. http://www.saltspring. com/capewest/ct.htm

Spencer S. Eccles Health Sciences Library, University of Utah, Sharon Dennis (1998). http://medlib.med.utah.edu/

University of Buffalo (1997). Case Studies in Science Collection. http://ubli9b.buffalo.edu/libraries/projects/cases/ubcase.htm

University of Delaware (1999). Problem-Based Learning. http://www.udel.edu/pbl/

Vernier Software, Vernier Software Company (2000). http://www.vernier.com

APPENDIX

INTERNET WEB SITES

The Internet sites listed here are Web sites we had visited when *Teaching Science in the Block* was written. We believe science teachers in the block will find some of the sites useful. We also realize and remind readers that the sites listed may change over time. The sites were chosen because they were easy to navigate and provided information and activities determined to be useful. The sites should serve as samples and/or examples only; no attempt was made to locate and review all of the relevant sites available.

GENERAL SCIENCE SITES

1. National Science Teachers Association:
   http://www.nsta.org/

   A site designed to promote excellence and innovation in science teaching and learning for all.

2. Smithsonian National Air and Space Museum:
   http://www.nasm.si.edu/

   A site containing information about the National Air and Space Museum and science instruction.

3. Gateway to Educational Materials (GEM):
   http://www.thegateway.org/

   A consortium effort to provide educators with quick and easy access to the substantial, but uncataloged, collections of educational materials found on various federal, state, university, nonprofit, and commercial Internet sites. Use the search engine or click on "Browse subjects" to reach a menu whose "science" item breaks out into 30 subcategories. ERIC Clearinghouse on Information & Technology

4. Anthro Limited:
   http://www.athro.com/

   The Athro Limited Web publishes interactive exercises in biology, earth science, and geology for high school and college students.

5. Awesome Library:
   http://www.awesomelibrary.org

   Provides a list of over 100 lesson plans and projects for various grade levels and areas of science. Also includes links to other Web pages, categorized by area of science (botany, chemistry, biology, et al.)

6. Study Guides and Strategies:
   www.iss.stthomas.edu/studyguides

   Study Guides and Strategies, an online manual, can help students learn how to learn. The site gives tips on note taking, test taking, reading skills, studying, writing essays, and more. This for any student, not specifically a science student.

7. Ask the Experts:
   www.sciam.com/askexpert/index.html

   Scientific American's conduit to experts on all fields of science has links to all their experts in one place. This site is a good resource for students and teachers. Question-and-answer format.

8. Lesson Plan Links by Classroom Connect:
   Rrnet.com/~gleason/lesson.html

   The Lesson Plan Link has lots of lesson plans. For science-related lessons, go to the subject listing.

BIOLOGY

1. Access Excellence:
   http://www.accessexcellence.org

   Genentech, Inc.'s national program to put high school biology teachers in touch with their colleagues.

2. MIT Biology Hypertextbook:
   http://esg-www.mit.edu:8001/esgbio/ 7001main.html

   Contains Chapters on all biology topics (Chemistry Review, Large Molecules, Cell Biology, Enzyme Biochemistry, etc.), a biology syllabus, and practice problems.

3. The Virtual Cell Web Page:
   http://personal.tmlp.com/Jimr57/index.htm

   Take a complete tour of interactive cell. Contains topics in biology, chemistry, math, and physics.

4. The Human Genome Project Information:
    http://www.ornl.gov/TechResources/Human_Genome/home.html

    This Website is maintained by the Human Genome Management Information System (HGMIS) at the Oak Ridge National Laboratory for the U.S. Department of Energy Human Genome Program.

CHEMISTRY

1. BioChemNet:
    http://schmidel.com/bionet.cfm

    A guide to Biology and Chemistry Educational Resources on the Web. Contains:
    - General Biology
    - General Chemistry
    - Organic Chemistry
    - Biochemistry
    - Molecular Genetics
    - Teaching Science
    - Science Careers
    - Science Clip Art
    - Science News and Journals

2. Chemicool:
    http://www.chemicool.com/

    An interactive Periodic Table of the Elements containing detailed information on each element.

3. General Chemistry Online!:
    http://antoine.frostburg.edu/chem/senese/101/

    Includes interactive course guides and tutorials, an exam survival guide, reference tables, self-grading quizzes and exams, a searchable glossary, a question-and-answer board, answers to over 300 frequently asked questions, and a chemical trivia quiz. Created by Dr. Fred Senese, chemistry professor at Frostburg State University in Maryland.

4. NIST Chemistry Web Book:
    http://webbook.nist.gov/chemistry/

    Includes thermodynamic data for over 5000 chemical compounds and ion-energetics data for over 10000 chemical compounds.

5. World Chemistry Interactive:
   http://www.wbaileynet.com/wldchem/home/index.htm

   Comprehensive chemistry resource for upper-level chemistry students.

EARTH SCIENCE

1. Global Volcanism Program:
   http://www.volcano.si.edu/gvp/

   Volcanic activity reports, large volcanoes of the world database, and comprehensive links to other volcano sites.

2. Living in the Learning Web:
   http://www.usgs.gov/education/living/index.html

   Provides information on earth science topics that affect daily life, including household water, weather's effects on streams, and preparing for volcanic eruptions.

3. The Mineral Gallery:
   http://mineral.galleries.com/default.htm

   Searchable by name, class, groupings, or keyword.

4. Smithsonian Gem & Mineral Collection:
   http://galaxy.einet.net/images/gems/gems-icons.html

   Photographs of many minerals and gems found in the Smithsonian collection.

5. This Dynamic Earth: the story of Plate Tectonics:
   http://pubs.usgs.gov/publications/text/dynamic.html

   Online edition of a 1996 book from the United States Geological Survey (USGS)

6. Volcanoes Online:
   http://library.thinkquest.org/17457/

   A spectacular site on volcanoes and plate tectonics

7. Volcano World:
   http://volcano.und.nodak.edu/

   Pictures, videos, links, and lots of other information about volcanoes.

8. TopoZone—The Web's Topographic Map:
   http://www.topozone.com/

   The TopoZone is the Web's center for topographic map users and outdoor recreation enthusiasts. We've worked with the USGS to create the Web's first interactive topo map of the entire United

States. If you're looking for maps that don't leave big blank spaces between the highways.

9. National Oceanic and Atmospehric Administration (NOAA):
   http://www.noaa.gov/

   Links to weather, El Nino, and environmental information.

10. UM Weather (Weather Underground):
    http://ww2010.atmos.uiuc.edu/(Gh)/guides/mtr/home.rxml

    The heart of the site is the Weather Underground database of weather conditions and forecasts from around the globe and links to more than 380 weather sites in North America; weather cams that take live pictures of current weather conditions in over 800 locations; tropical storm-related sites; radar and satellite imagery; and temperature, jet-stream, and upper-air maps.

11. Weather: What forces affect our weather?:
    http://www.learner.org/exhibits/weather/

    Explore the forces behind the weather, try yourr hand at tornado chasing, or discover how wind chill works. Hands-on activities include topics such as the atmosphere, the water cycle, ice and snow, and forecasting. Produced by the Annenberg/CPB Collection.

12. NASA:
    http://www.nasa.gov/

    Educational opportunities and information avaliable from NASA.

ENVIRONMENTAL AND ECOLOGICAL INFORMATION

1. EE-Link:
   http://nceet.snre.umich.edu/

   Environmental education resource for K–12 teachers with activities, lessons, contacts, links to organizations and projects, and regional information related to the environment.

2. EPA's Global Warming Page: State by State Impacts:
   http://www.epa.gov/globalwarming/impacts/stateimp/index.html

   Includes impacts of global warming on other ecosystems.

3. EPA's Surf Your Watershed:
   http://www.epa.gov/surf/

   Detailed information about our watersheds.

4. Garbage: How Can My Community Reduce Waste:
   http://www.learner.org/exhibits/garbage/

   An online interactive exhibit from the Annenberg/CPB Project.

5. The Nature Conservancy:
    http://www.tnc.org/

6. Paul Ehrlich and the Population Bomb:
    http://www.pbs.org/kqed/population_bomb/

    Examines Paul Ehrlich's theories about overpopulation and a range
    of global problems. Includes current statistics, directory of organi-
    zations, glossary, population timeline, and more.

7. PlanetDiary:
    http://www.phschool.com/science/planetdiary/

    Records the events and phenomena that affect Earth and its resi-
    dents. Every week, this site presents geological, astronomical, mete-
    orological, biological, and environmental news from around the
    globe.

8. Virtual Galapagos:
    http://www.terraquest.com/galapagos/index.html

    Explore the Galapagos Islands with a group of writers, scientists,
    and photographers.

PHYSICS

1. Amusement park physics: the roller coaster:
    http://www.learner.org/exhibits/parkphysics/coaster.html

    An Annenberg/CPB exhibit that presents the history and physics of
    roller coasters and provides opportunities for designing a roller
    coaster.

2. Cornell Theory Center math and Science Gateway—Physics:
    http://www.tc.cornell.edu/Edu/MathSciGateway/physics.html

    Links to a powerful assortment of physics sites.

3. The Laws List:
    http://www.alcyone.com/max/physics/laws/index.html

    Laws, rules, principles, effects, paradoxes, limits, constants, experi-
    ments, and thought- experiments in physics.

4. The Particle Adventure:
    http://ParticleAdventure.org/

    An interactive tour of the inner workings of the atom and the tools
    of discovery.

5. Physics 2000:
    http://www.Colorado.EDU/physics/2000/index.pl

    An interactive journey through modern physics.

6. PhysLINK: The Ultimate Physics Resource:
   http://www.physlink.com/

   Physics reference, societies, and publications, with links to history,
   news, and fun physics sites

7. Roller Coaster Physics by Tony Wayne:
   http://www.pen.k12.va.us/Anthology/Pav/Science/Physics/
   book/ home.html

   Explains principles in design of roller coasters.

8. Theater of Electricity:
   http://www.mos.org/sln/toe/toe.html

   An overview of how electricity works and a look at the historical
   use of electricity in scientific experiments from Boston's Museum of
   Science. Includes information on Tesla coils, Van deGraaff genera-
   tors, and Ben Franklin's kite experiments.

9. Computer Animations of Physical Processes:
   http://www.infoline.ru/g23/5495

   This physics site offers animated experiments on and visualizations
   of waves, optics, and more. Explanations included.